# ELEVATING
# CO-TEACHING
through **UDL**

# ELEVATING
# CO-TEACHING
### through UDL

## Elizabeth Stein

CAST Professional Publishing
UNTIL LEARNING HAS NO LIMITS™

Library of Congress Control Number: 2016944371

Paperback ISBN 978-1-930583-58-0
Ebook ISBN 978-1-930583-59-7
Library ISBN 978-1-930583-72-6

Published by:
CAST Professional Publishing
an imprint of CAST, Inc.
Wakefield, Massachusetts, USA

Author photograph by Angela Dee

For information about special discounts for bulk purchases, please contact publishing@cast.org or telephone 781-245-2212 or visit www.castpublishing.org

Cover and interior design by Happenstance Type-O-Rama.

Printed in the United States of America.

*For educators everywhere—*
*including parents, teachers,*
*administrators, students and*
*peers—who value and advocate*
*for the unique talents, expertise,*
*and abilities of each other.*

# Contents

# Introduction: Embracing the Co-teaching Experience

CO-TEACHING—MEANINGFUL AND GENUINELY AUTHENTIC CO-TEACHING—IS NOT A JOB FOR THOSE WHO WANT TO TAKE THE EASY ROUTE. Since I began my co-teaching career 25 years ago, oh, the stories I could tell! My experiences range from the ideal to the extremely flawed. And I cherish each experience, because each served to be a valuable learning experience that has shaped who I am as an educator. I have translated my experiences into a more-developed mission with a magnified passion and deeper sense to do whatever it takes to advocate for students.

Co-teaching is not always an easy position to be in—especially if one of the co-teachers is not on board with cooperation and collaboration. At the same time, co-teaching is one of the most rewarding experiences any teacher could have. There is always something to learn—and there is always more than one way of learning and teaching. Over the years, I have developed a co-teaching mantra: *Co-teaching is not a teaching assignment—co-teaching is a teaching experience.*

Every co-teaching encounter is part of a learning process for all involved. When we allow ourselves to "go with the flow" and experience the ups and downs, along with the celebrations and the frustrations, we are open to embracing a solution-seeking mindset because we are immersed in experiencing co-teaching—come what may. When we experience co-teaching, we learn to take all situations in stride as part of a process as we keep the strengths and needs of our students clearly in sight. Our minds remain open and flexible, our thinking persists proactively and responsively, and our focus is set on our mission to provide the absolute best learning process for our students. And this focus is a stabilizing rock, so when we encounter those inevitable setbacks, that's just fine—they're just bumps in the road.

In the past decade, Universal Design for Learning (UDL) has helped me put students first—no matter what my co-teaching situation happened to be—and to keep my vision clear through the process of designing instruction so that the strengths and needs of students remained a central concern. UDL allowed me to experience every co-teaching situation. UDL became my cushion to fall back on any time I needed to regroup and refocus on the most important factor: student connections and personal achievements. When co-teachers relax into their co-teaching assignments, they are ready to learn something new, share their ideas, and work together to co-create learning environments that allow all learners (including the two teachers!) to experience learning as the meaningful process it should be.

In my first year of teaching in the early 1990s, I had to work with two classroom aides, parents, speech and language teachers, occupational therapists, physical therapists, and behavior specialists. The class was composed of students with autism with a range of abilities. All of the educators worked together closely to give these students every opportunity to achieve at their absolute personal best. As the teacher, I needed to make decisions that affected everyone in the room. I included the opinions, talents, and ideas from all educators who worked closely with the students. Many of the students in the classroom did not communicate with verbal language. We created communication boards (with laminated Velcro pictures—no computers back then!), and designed activities that provided opportunities for each student to express himself or herself. Students expressed themselves through pointing, dancing, smiling, nodding, or speaking. We, as a community of learners in our classroom, created an environment that allowed everyone to experience the concepts that we needed to teach.

This original poster (all tattered and loved) was given to me by a parent—it expresses the essence of our UDL mind-sets that year (Fig. I.1). We just didn't know it was UDL at the time! We co-created a learning environment that provided the opportunity for everyone in the room to experience learning in a risk-free, motivating environment. Each student had the opportunity to express his or her thoughts, feelings, and responses. Learning was not a chore or checklist of skills to learn and accomplish—it was an experience that created relationships with all educators and students, and with the learning process itself.

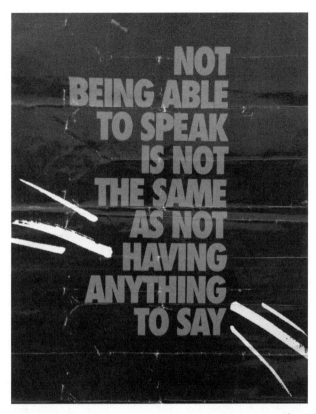

**FIGURE I.1.** Poster by Rosemary Crossley, educator and founder of DEAL Communication Centre, Melbourne, Australia. (Created by the Division of Special Education and Rehabilitation, in Syracuse, New York)

As co-teachers, we must agree to join in a process of learning—learning together as teachers and learning with our students as we pave the way for meaningful learning to unfold. Co-teaching can become so much more than just co-creating relationships and opportunities to experience learning. Imagine the ideal inclusive classroom setting where all students' thoughts are valued, all students' strengths are embraced, and all students' needs are met along a clear path that embraces individual strengths and allows learners to immerse themselves in the process of true learning.

My hope is that throughout this book, readers will have the opportunity to connect and to realize that this vision can come to fruition in their classrooms. Universal Design for Learning can become an educator's mind-set that results in positive, meaningful learning environments for all students. In addition, students with disabilities, English language learners, and gifted and talented students may feel empowered in general education settings when provided with the right opportunities for creating personal learning experiences, thus allowing them to make ongoing progress toward achieving their personal best. This book will provide strategies and action steps co-teachers can take to create successful learning environments for all students.

Two promises are held within the pages of this book. The first is to inform you, the reader, about the power that a UDL approach can have on any learning environment. The second is that a deeper understanding of UDL will ignite your connections, transform your thinking, and activate your ideas for specific ways to elevate instruction. Yes, I know—those are big promises to fulfill. But UDL offers a means to fulfill them. Just keep an open mind to the possibilities.

## WHO THIS BOOK IS FOR

Preservice and novice teachers will gain the background to be knowledgeable, while being inspired to adopt and implement a UDL mind-set in their future classrooms. Veteran teachers, university professors, and administrators will begin to naturally connect to what they already know, as well as learn new ideas and tools to instill a passion for learning within a barrier-free environment. This book is for new and veteran teachers who are ready to hit the ground running in UDL style. It is also a book for college professors and supervisors to use as they share the knowledge and necessity for student teachers to understand how to proactively plan and differentiate their lessons with precision to meet the diverse needs of students in inclusive settings.

## WHAT THIS BOOK PROVIDES

This book will provide a foundation in key UDL ideas that need to be considered before we dive into practical strategies and routines to elevate the co-teaching in any inclusive classroom setting. In basic terms, UDL is a framework of principles and guidelines for designing curriculum and instruction that connects learners with the learning process in meaningful ways. To put it another way, UDL is a method of thinking that proactively anticipates and plans for the needs of diverse individuals. In the learning environment, teachers' mind-sets and their philosophical beliefs about how children learn are part of the necessary process for creating a clear path between students of all ability levels and the content itself. Teachers must think about what it is they have to teach and connect it with the strengths and needs of the learners in their room. These chapters discuss practical options for accomplishing this.

This book will have tips and strategies that can be used in classrooms right away. In fact, I steer away from technical research, definitions, and descriptions, and dive right into the practical applications. This is a book for teachers who want to engage their students in meaningful learning within the moments of class and far beyond those moments. This is a book for teachers who have the privilege of working with a co-teacher and finding ways to maximize the expertise, knowledge, and talents of each other. It's a book for all those educators who continually ask themselves, "What can I do for children?" and who continually stay focused on their journey to find ways to do it. UDL has been the way for me—and I am so honored to be sharing my passion with you. There's something here for everyone!

## HOW THIS BOOK IS ORGANIZED

The chapters in this book are structured in a way that provides opportunities for readers to apply UDL within the structure of their lessons. Part 1 (Chapters 1–3) offers a foundation of important ideas. Part 2 (Chapters 4–7) introduces teachers to a workshop view as they begin to think about how to meaningfully connect to, reflect on, and apply UDL to elevate instruction in their co-teaching world.

So be prepared to experience a potentially powerful mind-set shift—it's all up to you! Let's begin by considering what it takes to create learning environments for students in co-taught classrooms. Allow your thinking to go deeper as you begin to look through a UDL lens. We'll start by taking a peek into two co-taught classrooms in Anywhere, U.S.A. So buckle up! Let our co-teaching with UDL journey begin. . .

# ELEVATING
# CO-TEACHING
### through UDL

# PART

# 1

# Understanding Co-teaching through the Lens of Universal Design for Learning (UDL)

# Transform Co-teaching Approaches with Universal Design for Learning

LET'S STEP BACK IN TIME FOR A MOMENT. It will just take a second for us to go back to my first experience working as a co-teacher—here's how it began...

I entered the classroom to meet my co-teacher. She was busy filing some papers and organizing some books on a shelf. As I walked in and introduced myself (all smiles, extended hand), she looked up from her books, tilted her head to allow herself to glance at me from the tips of her glasses, and said, "Hi, it's nice to meet you."

She shook my hand in an obligatory fashion—with less than two seconds of eye contact and a loose grip—then went back to filing and shelving. She responded to comments and questions I posed, and she asked me a few questions as a gesture to get to know me as well—yet I couldn't help but feel like I was in the way. I was invading her space. Her tone, her body language, and her complete indifference was felt and seen. Without speaking, she made it clear she had greater things to do—more important people to speak with—and I knew she wanted to be anywhere but there, with me.

When the air became too thick for either one of us to chisel through, I said, "Well, it was very nice to meet you, and I am looking forward to working with you this year." I wasn't lying—I meant every word. But I was a bit deflated. My vision of collaboration and co-teaching were not following the smooth pathway I envisioned. As I was walking out, she called me back into the room.

Here's what she said: "I'm sorry if I do not seem as enthusiastic as you do—this is my third year co-teaching, and the first two years left me feeling very discouraged. I worked with the same co-teacher the last two years, and it didn't work out.

It wasn't her fault—or my fault—the system got in the way. She was often pulled for meetings and we never had any time to plan together. It was so overwhelming to guide struggling learners through grade-level expectations. It's just heartbreaking. Maybe you're right that this will be a good year for us—but I wouldn't count on it if I were you."

My view of co-teaching broadened tremendously in those moments. I interpreted her ability to disclose her thoughts and experiences to me as a positive sign that we would work very well together. After all, my hope for open and ongoing communication had already begun—and it was only the first day!

## COMMON CHALLENGES IN CO-TEACHING

Co-teaching has been practiced for many, many decades. Yet the same problems persist: nonexistent communication routines, a lack of common planning time, differences in teaching styles and knowledge, scheduling glitches, and difficulties meeting the needs of diverse learners. So why do some co-teaching pairs work successfully? Many argue that co-teachers must stay together over time to make it work. But I argue that our students don't have time for that. We must make it work *now*. *This* year. For *this* group of students. It is also unrealistic to think that co-teacher dyads can be scheduled together each year. We must turn our minds to seeking solutions. What can *we do* now? We must identify a way to make co-teaching—any co-teaching pairing—work, no matter what.

As we begin to identify surefire ways to make co-teaching work, let's visit two classrooms.

Enter co-taught classroom #1. Any grade—any subject—anywhere. Focus Anchor Standard: *Determine central ideas or themes of a text and analyze their development; summarize the key supporting details and ideas.* This class of 25 students is sitting in rows listening to one of the teachers read aloud from a chapter book. The teacher walks up and down the rows as she dramatically reads and makes eye contact with each student. She uses her voice to guide students to visualize character traits and story elements. She pauses every so often to remind students to close their eyes and visualize. There are no external visuals. There are no additional materials. Just one teacher, rows of desks, and students sitting at their desks encouraged to use their imaginations. The students are visibly attentive as they watch the teacher read with some dramatic displays of expression and voice. A few chuckles can be heard around the room as she reads.

The second co-teacher at the back of the room follows along in her copy of the book, ready to take over the reading as the first teacher nods and smiles her way. Before this second teacher reads, she asks the students a few guided questions to make sure they are following along and understand what's happening in the text so far. These questions are orally presented to the entire class. There are no visuals and no additional materials.

The students are still sitting in their seats. This teacher also walks around the room, so all of the students are once again seemingly attentive. A few students eagerly raise their hands. Some quickly look down at their shoes as the teacher walks past their desk. One or two students are called on, the answers to the comprehension questions are revealed, and the teacher succinctly sums up what has happened in the reading so far. She is ready to continue reading. Students once again follow the teacher's movements and smile as she, too, reads with dramatic expression. At the end of the reading, the first teacher says, "Great class today! Be ready for a quiz on this chapter at the beginning of our next class." The teacher quickly directs the class to transition to the next subject.

Now let's enter co-taught classroom #2 to see the same lesson. The class of 25 students is sitting in groups of five. Students' desks are facing one another. The first teacher is up at the SMART Board reviewing some active reading strategies. She opens a discussion on how to annotate the text to deepen the readers' comprehension. The second co-teacher takes the lead and tells the class they will be practicing this annotation skill during the reading of a short paragraph, as she models her thinking and annotating.

The first co-teacher asks each group to discuss what they noticed about the teacher's think-aloud and how it connected to their own thinking. Students are given a few minutes to discuss. Following a quick debriefing, the first co-teacher introduces the text they were about to read. She offers students a choice. They can read the text while following along with text-to-speech software, they can engage in a shared reading with one of the teachers reading aloud, they can use iPads to read the text electronically (and benefit from dictionary apps), they can partner-read with a peer, or they can choose to go solo and read silently. This may sound like a lot of choices, but these students are used to making decisions about how they will learn best. Their opinions, feelings, moods, and voice are valued each day.

The classroom is set up for the ease of arranging desks and students have the flexibility to choose the process for engaging in the learning experience. As the students move seamlessly around the room, they are ready to begin the reading task within a few minutes. Assigning student groups is not necessary. Thirteen students choose to go solo and complete the reading assignment successfully on their own, while using the iPads occasionally to support their vocabulary knowledge. Five students sit in a group, with one of the co-teachers reading as they follow along. Two students choose to partner-read, whereas five students choose to go to the computer lab, where the librarian has set them up to read along using Google text-to-speech supports. The second co-teacher is monitoring the engagement of all students and implementing supports, as needed. She notices that all students are engaged and taking charge of their own learning.

There you have it: two co-taught classrooms implementing the same lesson in two completely different styles. These two classrooms unveil many challenges experienced in any co-taught classroom. And they also reveal many possible solutions.

What is your first impression? Are both classrooms applying effective instruction? Why do you think the way you do? Are you able to identify the co-teaching models of instruction in each classroom? Are you able to identify the UDL components?

Regardless of where you are in your understanding of UDL and co-teaching, jot down your initial thoughts here:

*First Impressions*

*Evidence of effective instruction in both classrooms:*

_____

_____

*Evidence of co-teaching models:*

_____

_____

*Evidence of UDL components:*

_____

_____

We will return to this reflective discussion in Chapter 6, "Empowering Students as UDL Partners," but don't look ahead—that will just ruin all the fun! As you read through the pages of this book, you will gain a deeper perspective into ways to describe what is happening in each classroom. Allow yourself to visualize and to connect to classrooms you know. And equally as important, allow the text to spark ideas for creating inclusive co-taught classrooms that work—no matter what.

It's not a secret—some co-teachers get along beautifully, while often, far too many do not. The roadblocks to effective co-teaching experiences can fall into these two categories:

1. Instruction

   • Dealing with differences in content knowledge and teaching styles

   • Meeting the needs of diverse learners

2. Communication

   • Identifying ongoing communication methods

   • Creating a realistic common planning routine

Co-teachers often do not agree on instructional and classroom management approaches. Each teacher brings a level of knowledge and expertise that may not be valued by the other teacher, which often results in one teacher dominating the instructional scene. The general education teacher is often viewed as the content area specialist, which leaves the special education teacher worrying about stepping out of bounds.

The solutions to these roadblocks can become clear, and they expand possibilities for all learners. The possibilities extend so far and wide that the results can have a powerful ripple effect into the present and future success for all individuals in the classroom. It is not too good to be true. It is simply applying learning with integrity. The solutions to any co-teaching challenge can be found within these three perspectives and actions:

1. Embracing various co-teaching models

2. Embedding Universal Design for Learning (UDL)

3. Implementing deeper scaffolds through explicit instruction and specially designed instruction (SDI)

# ELEMENTS OF CO-TEACHING

Before we begin to discuss what instruction looks like, it's necessary to review a few basics. Too often inclusion and co-teaching are used synonymously. We hear statements such as, "I'm an inclusion teacher;" "My child is in the inclusion class;" "These are inclusion students." This is just plain wrong. There is no such thing as an inclusion class, inclusion students, or an inclusion teacher. Inclusion is not a place or a program. It is not a way to describe students, a teacher, or a class. Inclusion is an idea and a philosophy. It is a belief system that embraces the reality that diverse individuals are included within a positive learning environment. Co-teaching, on the other hand, is a service delivery as a means to provide students with additional scaffolds, supports, and specialized instruction within the general education setting (Friend, 2014). Inclusive settings embrace the variable needs of learners, and students' needs are met within the delivery of a co-teaching model.

A couple of key components are always visible in the most successful co-taught inclusive settings:

**A shared vision exists.** Each teacher is connected with his or her personal philosophy and beliefs about what is right for students. With this solid, personal understanding, each teacher must be open to the perspective of the other teacher. When philosophies are in sync and naturally aligned, life is beautiful and a smooth road to co-teaching is clearly paved. However, co-teachers who have different beliefs can also share a vision and focus by communicating their personal beliefs and discussing ways to create a clear path. Active listening, communication, and compromise are essential for a successful learning environment. (See the Co-teaching Shared Vision Planning Page in this book's appendix.

**Active expertise from both teachers is evident.** General education and special education teachers have shared, as well as unique qualities that must be nurtured and present throughout the school year. Figure 1.1 depicts the uniqueness and the overlap of the areas of expertise.

As we think about current trends as well as the future of education, it is not too difficult to see that the distinguishing line between general education and special education begins to blur. All teachers need to align the deep learning through a rigorous and exciting curriculum and ensure that we are guiding and supporting our students for a successful future.

General education teachers need to have some of the qualities that a special education teacher possesses. For example, general education teachers must become savvy, with a repertoire of strategies that can meet the needs of diverse learners. In addition, they must have the understanding, tools, and ability to apply progress monitoring techniques to guide meaningful learning for all students. Special education teachers must have the content knowledge to be able to implement high-quality instruction within the framework of initiatives such as Common Core, as well as the ability to apply effective classroom management skills within the co-taught classroom. And so, it is no secret—we need one another. Collaboration, respect, and ongoing communication are necessary to ensure that each teacher is committed to the learning journey in the classroom.

### Expertise of General Education Teacher

- Process of learning/strategy expert
- Individualizing/differentiating instruction
- Small group/behavior management
- Data collection/progress monitoring
- Emphasis on master of skills not coverage of content and pacing

### Expertise of General Education Teacher

- Content knowledge
- Classroom management
- Understanding of typical learners
- Pacing of general education curriculum guides, materials, and grade level expectations

**FIGURE 1.1.** Balancing different expertise

# SIX CO-TEACHING MODELS

A classroom has the potential to ignite the learning for everyone—including the teachers. There is a balance of teacher-directed and student-directed learning that flows within the structure of six specific co-teaching approaches (Friend & Cook, 2007). Within the framework of learning, the student is at the center of it all. Teachers decide which model will best meet the academic, social, and emotional needs of students within the context of a specific lesson. Co-teachers should keep in mind the value of considering the need to vary small groups and whole-class learning. This flowing movement of the models has great potential to keep students engaged and connected to the learning moments.

## One Teaches, One Observes

One teacher manages the instruction, while the other teacher organizes and implements specific assessment tools to gather data on students' performance. This model should be used occasionally as the need arises.

### Example

During a seventh-grade social studies class, Nick intermittently shuts down. He puts his head on the desk and often speaks in a low voice: "I just can't do this." The general education teacher handles this by ignoring him or asking him to sit up. The special education teacher does not want to draw negative attention to the student's behaviors and often just speaks with him one on one during and after class to get him back on track.

### Benefits

As one teacher instructs the whole class, the other teacher could complete an ABC analysis to identify the **a**ntecedents, **b**ehaviors, the **c**onsequences. In time, the teachers may analyze the data to identify patterns in activities or student behaviors as a means of effectively addressing and redirecting students within the moments of class time. For example, they may notice that Nick shuts down anytime there is going to be group work or a writing task. With this evidence, the teachers will be able to proactively plan and effectively reduce Nick's disengaged and disruptive behaviors and redirect toward successful social and academic learning behaviors. This model should be used occasionally while both teachers remain mindful that they are active participants with expertise that must be valued.

## Station Teaching

This model has great potential because both teachers share their expertise and teaching responsibilities. It also allows both teachers to plan for the learner variability that exists in every classroom. The benefits of station teaching include the ability to:

- Apply flexible grouping depending on the content and activities

- Create groups that focus on reteaching or preteaching

- Plan for groups based on students' skill level or interests

- Facilitate learning for one group, while another group works independently

### Example

In this eighth-grade classroom, one teacher facilitates a station to guide the students to gather and organize their notes on the causes of the Civil War. Students are provided with scaffolded support in their researching efforts. At the next station, another teacher guides the students to use their notes and text-based evidence to write an essay on the causes and effects of the Civil War. At this second station, students apply strategic thinking to add the details needed to write a well-written informative essay. The third station is an independent station where students work in pairs or independently to revise and edit their writing. Students also have the option to work solo at their desk to complete the task.

### Benefits

In this example, the benefits are varied. Students who are able to work independently have the option to work solo to express their skills and knowledge. Students who require support for the writing process are provided with explicit instruction to guide them toward independent researching and writing skills. Students rotate, as needed, between scaffolded supports and working independently to guide them through meaningful personal learning experiences. Other benefits to station teaching include the following:

- Teachers share content and apply their personal expertise.

- Students receive personalized, customized instruction.

- Students learn strategies and skills to guide them toward independence.

- Teachers can set up rotating stations, allowing all students to experience each station. Or stations may be set up as options for students to choose their learning process toward the same high expectations and learning outcomes.

## Parallel Teaching

The teachers divide the class into two groups and facilitate the same lesson with both groups. This model allows learners to receive a more individualized approach, while staying within the comfort of a large group. All learners receive instruction from one of the teachers without rotating groups. Each teacher can address the needs of the learners in manageable ways, and each learner has the opportunity to participate and have access to learning he may connect with personally.

### Example

In this third-grade class, the learners are directed to divide into two groups. One teacher calls out, "Okay, class, let's divide up—north side, go to the front of the room, and south side, meet at the back of the room." As the students move, the teachers wait for students to get settled. Each teacher is prepared to guide students to identify and label the continents on a world map. Although the objective is the same, the process of learning is adjusted to meet the needs of each group. One group uses iPads to give students the option of additional visual and kinesthetic input as they follow the teacher's discussion and map demonstration. Students are engaged by individually connecting to the content on their iPads as the learning unfolds. The other group gains the knowledge of the continents by watching and listening to the teacher's SMART Board demonstration. Students take turns interacting with the SMART Board as the group looks on and discusses the information as a group. By the end of the 45-minute lesson, all students have gained the knowledge necessary to identify and locate the seven continents.

## Benefits

This model is a very effective one that can be used frequently to meet the needs of all students. Both teachers are actively part of the instructional process and responsible for all students. Teachers have the ability to individualize instruction in meaningful ways since the group size is manageable. Both teachers have the flexibility to apply their teaching expertise. All students have the opportunity to personally access the learning material as they collaborate with the teacher and their peers during the learning process.

# Team Teaching

This model involves two teachers sharing the responsibility of the instruction throughout a lesson. Teaming should be used occasionally to guide whole-class learning, but co-teachers should avoid falling into the trap of both teachers taking on a general educator's role. The special education teacher must be sure to insert specially designed instruction whenever possible. Occasional application for team teaching is best since it may easily result in two teachers generally addressing students as a whole group. Teachers must be careful to make sure that each learner has the opportunity to access and generate meaning from the lesson activities. Each teacher takes on a role to be fully engaged in the delivery of the high-quality instruction.

## Example

In this seventh-grade science class, one teacher opens the lesson with a brief warm-up activity to get the class ready to learn about the phases of the moon. The warm-up activity requires the group to work in pairs to analyze a graphic that is up on the SMART Board screen. Students are required to simply jot down what they notice. The next teacher takes over and begins to apply the moon phase vocabulary to the students' observations. As one teacher speaks, the other adds comments to repeat or clarify concepts or vocabulary to ensure students' deeper comprehension skills. At the end of the teacher presentation, the students engage in an activity where they demonstrate their awareness of the various phases of the moon by matching a graphic with the specific vocabulary.

### Benefits

Teaming is a wonderful option for instruction if your goal is to show parity between the co-teachers during the instructional time. It is also beneficial for one teacher to clarify or repeat any important vocabulary or concepts needed for deeper comprehension. Teachers may model the process of learning as one teacher asks the other questions; this demonstrates to students that successful learners do ask lots of questions as they build their knowledge base. When used occasionally, this is a wonderful alternative that can keep the learning process novel and exciting.

## Alternative Teaching

This model is effective for times when some students need specialized attention. One teacher takes responsibility for teaching the large group while the other teacher facilitates learning for a small group. This small-group instruction may involve preteaching, reteaching, remediation, or just additional practice. The large group would be a review lesson or individual or group work that is fine for the small group to miss.

### Example

Ms. M. guides students to work in pairs to practice identifying text details to support their thinking in response to reading. As students work in pairs, Ms. M. provides additional supports as needed. Mr. G. works with a group of four students at a side table to reteach a strategy to guide students to deepen their independent comprehension skills.

### Benefits

This model should be implemented only occasionally and with careful thought. For starters, the same students should not be pulled to a small group all the time. The teachers may rotate who monitors the whole class and who provides direct instruction and additional practice in the small group. When implemented in this manner, students feel comfortable to receive additional support within a comfortable learning environment.

## One Teaches, One Assists

One teacher takes the lead for teaching the lesson while the other teacher monitors students' participation and understanding by circulating around the room. Students receive side-by-side additional support, as needed.

## Example

During this math lesson, one teacher is leading the class through the content. The other teacher walks around the room with a mini dry-erase board to review and reteach the concept as needed for individual students.

## Benefits

Students who need additional examples or explanations can receive this support. However, it can also be a distraction as one teacher and one student have a side conversation. In addition, as this additional support is being implemented, the student may fall behind on the whole-class lesson.

# CO-TEACHING MODELS AS A STARTING POINT

The co-teaching models ensure that each co-teacher's expertise will be valued and implemented. Yet the models alone do not work. Implementing a variety of co-teaching models means that learners are able to experience learning rather than just receive it by sitting passively within whole-class lessons. Each model of co-teaching creates opportunities for instruction to meet the needs of all students in the groups. Yet effective instructional strategies must be implemented. Let's look at one scenario.

In a seventh-grade classroom, the co-teachers decide to implement station teaching to guide students to read and take notes on the Columbian Exchange. Here's their plan:

*Station 1*: One co-teacher reviews one type of note-taking, models it for the group, and guides students to apply it to their own notebooks. The teacher scaffolds struggling learners to copy the model that she provides as a visual support.

*Station 2*: One co-teacher facilitates the reading of a section in the textbook to add to the students' background knowledge on the topic. Students who have difficulty reading are told to follow along as the teacher reads aloud. All other students may read silently on their own.

*Station* 3: Students work independently using laptops and complete a graphic organizer summarizing key points from their notes and reading so far.

These co-teachers are proud of their efforts to create active learning to meet the needs of all learners. It could be true that the smaller groups can serve to create more engaged learners—but have they created a more effective learning experience? Let's look at the first station, for instance. Students are guided to take efficient notes, but not only are students told *how* to take the notes, they are also encouraged to just copy from the teacher's model if they are having difficulty. How does just copying help learners be strategic, self-directed learners? The answer: it doesn't.

Clearly, it takes more than just applying co-teaching models when creating meaningful learning experiences. As the ideas in this book unfold, you will see that it is by combining co-teaching models, UDL and SDI, that will allow you to create relevant learning experiences for all learners in the room.

# TAKEAWAY IDEAS

- Inclusion is not a place or a program—it is not a way to describe a teacher, a student, or a type of class. Co-teaching is a service that is provided within a general education classroom to provide meaningful opportunities for all students to access the same high expectations within the general education curriculum.

- Use the expertise of both teachers.

- Varying the co-teaching models takes consideration and dedication to create active learning within small- and large-group experiences.

- Implementing the co-teaching models is a fabulous starting point—but not enough to make meaningful learning happen for each learner.

# STUDY GROUP QUESTIONS

1. What areas of expertise do you bring to the learning environment in your classroom? How does your expertise strengthen the learning process?

2. What areas of expertise does your co-teacher bring to the learning process? How can the two of you combine, embrace, and empower the learning moments through the power of two?

3. Share one lesson from the recent past and explain what co-teaching model(s) served to elevate the learning for teachers and students? How will you use the varied co-teaching models in a future lesson?

# 2

# Embrace Learner Variability the UDL Way

IT'S NO SECRET THAT DIVERSE LEARNERS ARE FOUND IN EVERY CLASS-ROOM, RIGHT? The need to differentiate instruction that meets the needs of our diverse students is common practice—and just common sense. So why are so many classroom teachers still scrambling to close students' personal learning gaps? It's easy to blame it solely on more rigorous standards, high expectations, or a lack of sufficient time and resources. But if we notice, observe, connect with, and focus on the students in front of us, then there is so much potential for meaningful learning to take place. Traditionally, teachers have been implementing differentiated instruction whenever possible. We provide additional supports for students who need it, but all too often students (far too many students!) fall out of our reach.

We are left with thoughts of, *How will I reach these students? Why isn't this student trying harder? What else can be done to help this student?* Well-intentioned teachers plan their instruction based on what they know a typical student in that grade level should be able to do. It's the traditional view of planning instruction down the middle—for the so-called average student. Once these teachers plan for this mythical middle, they may think they have taught the content simply because they exposed their students to the information. These teachers think they can pick up the pieces with a focus on providing extra help in hopes of "fixing" those students who are struggling. In addition, they may hope that the students who need more of a challenge will be inspired to do so on their own time. But why not create relevant, supportive, and challenging instruction within the moments of your class time? A teacher with a UDL mind-set does not need to worry about how to pick up the learning pieces for students after the lesson because UDL is all about planning the curriculum in ways that allow all students to access and meaningfully manipulate the content during instructional time. Fixing the curriculum is the focus—the focus is never about fixing the learner.

Let's consider a co-taught classroom—any classroom, with any two teachers. These teachers work hard to individualize the material to match students' specific needs. They soon find out this is a daunting task given the focus of the curriculum, the range of various learner needs, and the limitations to the resources they have available. During the process of their efforts, some students' needs are met. But with all due respect for the teachers' efforts, too many students (typically those who struggle the most) are just not learning.

When these teachers begin to proactively plan by looking at the curriculum and considering implementation through a UDL lens, they are able to predict specific points in the lessons and unit where barriers will exist between the students' strengths and needs and the content and process of learning itself. A whole new world is open for teachers and their students when instruction is proactively planned for systematic learner variability rather than trying to respond only to the needs of individual learners.

## SO WHAT EXACTLY IS LEARNER VARIABILITY?

Consider this: Would you offer the same textbook to a high school senior as you would to a fifth or sixth grader? Ridiculous! Of course not! This is because we already have this idea of systematic variability. We know that developmentally these students require different learning experiences based on their age.

As Todd Rose (http://udlseries.udlcenter.org/categories/explore.html) points out, we understand this known systematic variability to be called *development*. We accept the process of monitoring the developmental milestones of infants, toddlers, and school-aged children through this linear view to make sure they are within the range of healthy development. We hear children referred to as late (or early) walkers or talkers because of the age that they began to demonstrate that skill. There is a range of acceptability for when children may achieve these milestones. Yet there is this wish for achieving milestone skills by a desired point.

Similarly, using the deficit model to identify academic, social, and behavioral skills follows this view of expecting learners to fall into the range of what is thought of as average. The bell curve provides a strong visual to show how close or far from this mythical average a student performs. In so many cases (and the faces of many students come to mind here!), learners who fall short of what is viewed as average begin to believe that they are not smart enough or capable enough to join this group of "average" humans.

Parents, teachers, the students themselves, and society as a whole place a strong self-fulfilling prophecy on these learners. They then fall into the trap of not believing in their unique capabilities that could indeed guide them to reach levels of personal success. Thankfully, research and neuroscience have revealed the significance of yet another layer of systematic variability that is evident in any learning environment regardless of age of the learners. We can now begin to view learners through the lens of systematic variability—which highlights current brain research in support of neurodiversity and the fact that each brain is unique. Learners have a variety of strengths and needs that must be valued and nurtured in order for the individual to experience personal successes. This is learner variability—and it is the heart of UDL.

Learner variability explains why each year we have similar experiences with students. The faces of students change, yet we seem to have similar concerns and celebrations in reference to student learning. In addition, learner variability explains why year after year, teachers seem to be on a quest for strategies to motivate and engage the learners in their room. We hear similar gripes: "If only he would just apply himself;" "If only she would just do her homework;" "I don't know why he failed the math test, he was so attentive in class and he came for extra help." And here's a classic: "I always get the same students raising their hands." Another classic comment is, "She has a difficult home life with no support at home, so there's only so much I can do." But we must begin to take a deeper look into other factors.

Brain research supports the idea that the emotions play a huge role in setting the stage for learning. Brain research also supports our knowledge that we can predict the ways that all learners will be different (Meyer, Rose, and Gordon, 2014). We can begin to proactively plan for the variability in our classrooms as we think about upcoming lessons. And these differences are highly variable and highly acceptable from a strengths-based view, rather than a weakening deficit view.

This makes complete sense. Did you ever notice that year after year you have similar tales of woe when planning and implementing instruction? There are always those students who need more processing time. There are always those students who love to participate and express their ideas, and have their hand raised every chance they get. There are always those students who avoid a task and seem aloof (or even defiant). And there are always those students about whom we say, "I don't know what else I can do—but I need to do something."

Year after year, we strive to engage our students in the learning experiences we create. And year after year, we have similar experiences with the types of learners in our classroom (with the exception of highly individualized experiences). With this view of learner variability, we now know why. We are all different in the way we perceive, engage, and express our understanding. This is even true of adult learning—think about your last experience in a class or workshop. Learner variability exists any place where people come together to learn.

This is an extraordinary breakthrough for educators. It's a tremendously powerful view of designing learning experiences as we strive to guide learners to connect to learning. This is not something new or something additional for teachers to do. It is something that will serve to answer all our questions about what we can do to reach *each* learner in our classroom.

## VARIABILITY THROUGH THE UDL LENS

Take a moment to think about a class full of students. Notice the way the chairs, desks, and tables are set up. Notice the lighting and the time of day. What is the topic and general objective of the lesson? Notice the position of the teacher (maybe it's you!) in the room. What are the students doing? What is the teacher doing? Take a minute to write down or sketch your visualization here:

Here's my vision:

There are 30 students sitting in rows at individual desks. They are in social studies class learning about [*insert topic here*]. They are facing the teacher who is at the front of the class clicking away at the SMART Board to reveal a variety of facts through colorful images, videos, and bullet-point notes. The teacher asks a few questions—students volunteer to answer, and all students are directed to "take notes."

Okay, now that we have our visions, let's look at them in terms of the UDL principles of providing multiple means of engagement, action and expression, and representation (see Figure 2.1).

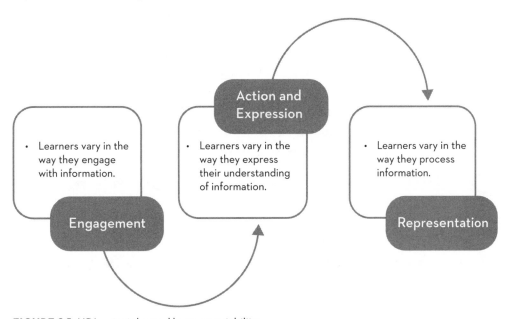

**FIGURE 2.1.** UDL principles and learner variability

Mapping my vision of the classroom to the principles, here's what I come up with:

**Engagement: Learners vary in the way they engage with the information.** This teacher has it covered. Or does he? He shares videos, visual images, text notes, and his own voice (auditory). But how are the students really connecting? Clearly some learners in that room have other things on their minds and are sitting at their desk quietly, passively listening and viewing, which is not working to gain meaningful attention. More needs to be considered to set a purpose and optimize motivation.

**Action and expression: Learners vary in the way they express their understanding.** The teacher aims to engage the class by tossing a few questions to the crowd. But you guessed it—the same students raise their hands. And the directive and expectation to "take notes" works well for less than half of this class. Others write random words on the page to make it look good, while many others do not take notes at all. More needs to be considered to guide each learner to be strategic, goal-directed, and dare I say, *organized* with note-taking!

**Representation: Learners vary in the way they process information.** This teacher can check off many effective ways to represent the information. He included video, audio, images, and texts, all on a colorful and prominent SMART Board presentation. But having multiple ways of representing information is not meant to be a checklist kind of process. More factors affect how we guide each learner to manipulate the information to create personal connections to guide transfer, generalizations, and ultimately make it to the background knowledge storehouse in their long-term memory.

Just think about what this knowledge of learner variability can mean to your classroom—or any classroom. Now take it a step further and think about students in the margins (Rose & Meyer, 2002)—that is, students with disabilities, English language learners, students who are gifted and talented, or anyone who does not fit in the big part of the bell curve. Through a UDL lens, teachers plan for variability, and not for some "average" student who does not really exist. Neuroscience has proven that learners are very different. There is no way to depict what an average student looks like since we know how different everyone is. Average is something that has been constructed based on historical views. It creates a situation where teachers plan instruction for the middle and hope that the students who are above or below average will be able to stay with the class.

However, many students are disconnected and way too much instructional time is lost. When teachers plan with a UDL lens and plan proactively for variability, those students in the margins are considered part of the variability, and they are not forced to fit into a lesson that is planned for this mythical middle. Lessons are planned for variability—and all students have the opportunity to connect to the learning process in personally meaningful ways.

All classrooms have variable learners, but inclusive classrooms unveil additional value to proactively planning for variability. Students will not be viewed by a label or category of disability or ability. Rather, they will blend naturally with their peers in ways that welcome individual strengths and needs. Students will connect to learning in the actual moments of instruction because their variability is part of the learning community in the classroom. Learning is a natural and accessible process because the teacher has a UDL mind-set leading toward student engagement, understanding, expression, and ultimately, student progress and achievement.

This knowledge of learner variability has additional value in a co-teaching setting. There is even greater variability within these inclusive settings. Teachers experience a great range of abilities each year. The opportunity of having two teachers in the room to notice and address the various needs must be maximized through the use of the co-teaching models, as well as applying the expertise of each teacher. In addition, incorporating a UDL mind-set can answer the question of how to reach such diverse learners. Viewing students as variable learners breaks down many academic and social barriers of categorizing learners into unnecessary groups based on learning deficits. With the belief in learner variability, teachers can design learning experiences that do not single out the struggling learners by creating a class within a class.

Co-teachers who understand learner variability will not have one teacher teaching the whole class while the other teacher is pulling the "struggling" learners to the back of the room. Rather, they will pay careful attention to the instructional structures, strategies, roles, and relationships they create and thereby set the stage for all learners to achieve their personal best and become expert learners.

## CULTIVATING EXPERT LEARNERS

Let's stay with this concept of the expert learner for a bit—a concept, incidentally, that applies to students and teachers alike, since we are all growing toward expertise. The word *expertise* brings to mind a sense of mastery, suggesting that experts have achieved a high-level mastery of knowledge and skills. Yet, as we consider expertise through the UDL lens, we open up our minds to a deeper sense of what this concept really means. We see learning as a process with a series of peaks and valleys that result in times when we struggle and times when we reach mastery of our learning targets. Learning is about the behaviors and the attitudes needed to connect during a personal, meaningful process that fosters a desire to keep learning. Learners are immersed in creating and following the action steps that lead to a desired outcome.

The process itself is motivating—the grade or end product is not the sole source of satisfaction. The drive to learn is not about reaching the end result alone—the product or outcome is only meaningful when the process provides opportunities for each learner to connect and push through any obstacles or struggles in order to reach a learning target. The process is what provides the learners with the knowledge and skills they need in order to learn anything, any-time—and every time.

Educators have an important role in teaching students to be expert learners—teaching each student to be the best version of themselves for these moments in time. Expert learners take charge of their own learning; they are responsible for identifying a purpose, creating and implementing an action plan, and monitoring their learning in ways that keep them on a continuous learning journey by adding new knowledge.

For example, Nick and Jordon enter seventh grade with high expectations for themselves. They have a history of struggling through school. They both start the year off overwhelmed with their new schedules, and the amount of homework, books, and content to remember. They both attend extra help sessions to practice skills, subjects, and organization of materials and note-taking. As the year moves along, both boys continue to fail many tests. They have a difficult time keeping up with assignments. By March, Jordon has stopped trying. His locker is equivalent to the hallway trash can—and he's lost a few of his textbooks.

Nick has stayed the course. He continues to attend extra help sessions, and he independently applies a note-taking strategy that was taught to him earlier in the year. Nick's grades do not always match his efforts and thought-ful, strategic learning process, but he enjoys school and loves to learn, and he has gained a newfound interest in learning about history and science. His parents are not pleased with his failing grades but admit they see a "new kid."

After receiving a failing grade, Nick makes test corrections and identifies a strategy that could help him study and transfer the information next time. Over time, Nick has demonstrated his true expert learning abilities. He has a clear purpose for learning that motivates him to gain the knowledge and seek the resources he needs. In addition, he identifies strategies that work for him to achieve his goals.

In any classroom, but particularly in a co-taught classroom, teachers can create expert learners who go way beyond what a grade on a test, assignment, or report card states. According to the UDL Guidelines (Meyer, Rose, & Gordon, 2014), an expert learner is resourceful and knowledgeable, strategic and goal-oriented, and purposeful and motivated. (See Table 2.1 for the characteristics of expert learners.)

**TABLE 2.1.** Characteristics of Expert Learners through the UDL Lens

| LEARNERS WHO ARE ENGAGED ARE: | LEARNERS WHO GAIN MEANING FROM THEIR PERCEPTIONS ARE ABLE TO: | LEARNERS WHO SET GOALS AND CREATE AN ACTION PLAN ARE ABLE TO: |
|---|---|---|
| Purposeful and motivated | Be resourceful and knowledgeable | Identify and apply strategies to organize information |
| Eager to learn and motivated by the process of reaching the outcome | Tap into their background knowledge base to build upon new knowledge | Monitor their performance throughout the learning experience |
| Goal-directed—they have a vision for what the end result will be | Seek out and identify resources to help them gain new information | Decide which strategies work well and which strategies need adjustments to create positive learning experiences |
| Open to pushing themselves beyond their comfort zones and challenging themselves to learn more | Deepen their understandings by connecting known information with new information | |
| Resilient and encouraged by the process of learning, and see setbacks as a natural part of the learning process | | |
| Able to regulate their emotions so they can focus on a meaningful learning experience | | |

Source: CAST, 2011; Meyer, Rose, & Gordon, 2014. UDL Guidelines. Adapted with permission.

# CULTIVATING A GROWTH MIND-SET

As we think about learning as a process, we know that the experience will create a variety of emotions. There are times we feel satisfied, proud, and invigorated when our efforts lead to positive outcomes. We get the grade we want or the product looks like the vision we set out to create. Other times we become frustrated, discouraged, and possibly upset when the results do not meet our hopes or expectations. What constitutes learning? Is it when we have that final product to be proud of to prove, "Hey, I'm good at this!" Or is it the possible failing experience that provides the opportunity to truly learn as we reflect on mistakes and embrace the process of resilient effort that creates the most meaningful learning experiences?

We can all think of a time we succeeded easily at something—just as we can think of a time we struggled. Did you give up during that struggle—or persevere and stay strong to see the learning through? It's our mind-set that determines our learning experiences.

Stanford psychologist Carol Dweck (2006) defines mind-sets as the beliefs that individuals have about their abilities, intelligence, and overall qualities. She distinguishes between growth and fixed mind-sets. In a growth mind-set, learners believe that as long as they persevere through challenges, their efforts will result in their improving and learning. In a fixed mind-set, learners believe that their basic intelligence and abilities are static. They believe people are good at something or they're not—they see effort as a sign of weakness rather than as part of a natural learning experience. A fixed mind-set holds that people who succeed are talented. A growth mind-set does not deny talent exists but states that success happens through the efforts and perseverance.

Research supports that students with a growth mind-set perform better on challenging tasks than students with a fixed mind-set (Blackwell, Trzesniewski, & Dweck, 2007). It is important to note that all learners (all humans for that matter) do not simply hold either a growth or a fixed mind-set. We all experience a mixture of both as we go through daily learning experiences.

Mind-sets can be learned, practiced, and changed over time, as Dweck's research shows. Being mindful to practice a growth mind-set allows us to embrace the struggles that go along with meaningful learning experiences. When students are taught that the brain is a muscle that can be developed and in time can become smarter with effort and perseverance, students are intrinsically motivated to put forth their best efforts. Research also shows that the language parents and teachers use greatly influences students' mind-sets and performance (Dweck, 2006).

How does each co-teacher embrace effort and additional practice as part of a natural learning process? Making mind-set a part of discussions can provide valuable information as co-teachers develop class routines and policies that incorporate the values and beliefs of both teachers. For example, let's look at the following scenario.

Ms. A. and Mr. C. co-teach in a seventh-grade inclusive setting. Mr. C. is mainly concerned with covering the content and giving a test on Friday. Ms. A. knows that the pacing of the material covered along with the reading level presents barriers for many students to learn the content. Let's choose an ending to this scenario:

**Ending #1:** Ms. A. stays quiet, but provides extra help to students during their lunchtime. These students take the test on Friday and most earn a failing grade. Ms. A. then speaks to Mr. C. to share her thoughts that the class should be given an option to continue studying, make test corrections, and retake the test to show their growth. Mr. C. does not agree and says, "The material was taught, we have to move on—the students should have studied harder."

**Ending #2:** Ms. A. shares her thinking with Mr. C. She suggests that she incorporate additional scaffolds such as graphic organizers and video, and even have students role-play to demonstrate their understanding of the material. Mr. C. is hesitant because he is concerned about the time. They come to a compromise where scaffolds are added during the instructional time. The students take the test on Friday and most earn a failing grade. Ms. A. suggests that students should make test corrections, continue studying with specific strategies, and retake the test to show their growth. Mr. C. is hesitant, but remembers how engaged the students were in class. He discusses the situation with Ms. A., who reminds him that the students are becoming stronger at knowing how they learn and that this additional opportunity will not only boost their confidence and their content knowledge, but will strengthen their learning habits for future topics and experiences. Mr. C. sighs and trusts Ms. A.'s instincts. All students who received a failing grade are offered the opportunity to do test corrections and retake the test. All students who retake the test pass the test and become more motivated to learn the next topic.

Ending #1 clearly shows Mr. C.'s fixed mind-set as a barrier to guiding meaningful learning. Due to the lack of relationship-building between the two co-teachers,

Ms. A. tried to guide the students, but without a co-taught team approach, the students were forced into Mr. C.'s fixed mind-set world.

Ending #2 clearly shows how the power of communication between co-teachers can open worlds of opportunities for students. It may not be easy to create discussions when each co-teacher has a different perspective, but co-teachers must advocate for all learners in the room. Each teacher must be the voice for all learners, and also keep an open mind into different ways of guiding expert learners.

## GETTING TO KNOW OUR STUDENTS

The beginning of every school year is an exciting time when teachers plan activities to get to know their students. Interviews, checklists, and class activities are often implemented as everyone works to become a learning community that will set the tone for the year. Sometimes these interviews and inventories are completed and then filed away as the focus centers on the need to teach the content. As we take time in the beginning of the year to get to know our students, we must remember to continue developing our knowledge of our students, even when the pacing of the curriculum sweeps us into a whirlwind of content. In the co-taught classroom, there's an additional need to understand our students. Of course, learner variability exists in any classroom, anywhere. But students in an inclusive setting typically exhibit such a broad range of abilities that a higher level of planning and implementation is needed to ensure that we are meeting the needs of each student.

> ▶ ## Why I Don't Talk about Learning Styles
>
> Once we embrace the idea that all learners can become expert learners, we begin to realize that all meaningful learning is contextual. We learn to design lessons that encourage students to be flexible thinkers. We do not want to make assumptions (and create unnecessary and unintentional barriers!) by labeling our students as certain *types* of learners or by assuming that they have certain learning styles that determine whether they can become experts. Many teachers consider a student's "learning style" as they plan a lesson. Yet, as we have learned from the work of Daniel Willingham (2009), we can wonder whether learning styles exist at all. We know students have learning strengths—but to say that any particular learner is one fixed type of learner or another is a form of classifying students and interferes with a clear pathway to learning.

From a UDL perspective, meaningful learning happens within a context. So if we embrace a traditional learning-style approach and say that Tim is an auditory learner, his teachers—but more importantly, Tim himself—will consider this to be true. So in all his classes, his teachers are sure to provide additional auditory input. Yet by considering the learning style over the context of learning, well-intentioned teachers often create unintentional learning barriers.

For example, let's consider Tim in his sixth-grade English class. The text they are reading is supported by an audio CD to reinforce the comprehension for a few students in the class. That works out well for Tim. That same day, Tim goes to social studies class, and the teacher makes certain to provide additional auditory cues through her lecture and student discussions to reinforce students' understanding of the geography of the 13 colonies. Tim seems to understand the content. The next day, Tim is able to transfer his comprehension in English class, but he does not retain the information in social studies. The social studies teacher is heard speaking with the English teacher, "I don't get it, I provided additional auditory to support his understanding of the geography of the 13 colonies, and he is still struggling—maybe he didn't study enough. He will have to come for extra help at lunch."

From a UDL perspective, when the context of learning is considered, we realize that although learning style strengths are evident, it is the context that drives true learning. We need to consider what we are asking students to know and be able to do and provide learning pathways accordingly. In the case of the geography lesson, all Tim needed was additional visual to strengthen his understanding and transfer of the content—an additional map to view and a blank one to complete to guide deeper understanding. If additional visual and perhaps kinesthetic input had been provided in the moments of that lesson, Tim would not have needed to miss his lunch period to review content that was made unintentionally inaccessible during the moments of class time. It's all about the context of learning.

# Class Learning Profile

One effective tool for guiding a yearlong awareness and application of the knowledge of students' abilities and needs is the Class Learning Profile (adapted from Rose & Meyer, 2002), shown in Table 2.2 and the appendix. This is a powerful way to align the UDL principles into instruction in natural and meaningful ways as we look to educate the whole child. We teach individuals, not subjects. The class profile is an ideal tool for guiding our relationship with students throughout the year. The first column indicates the connection between learning and the three brain networks. The other columns outline the strengths, needs, and preferences as we look at individual students. This is a perfect co-teacher communication tool as well as a source for teachers to refer to as they proactively plan and implement lessons.

**TABLE 2.2.** Class Learning Profile

| NETWORK | STUDENTS' STRENGTHS | STUDENTS' NEEDS | GENERAL STUDENTS' PREFERENCES/ INTERESTS |
|---|---|---|---|
| **Affect**<br><br>The ability to push through and understand the purpose for learning along with ability to effectively integrate the emotions involved in learning | *William*: Focused<br><br>*Matthew*: Enjoys working independently<br><br>*Rachel*: Works well with peers<br><br>*Ted*: Asks meaningful questions<br><br>*Anthony*: Energetic | *William*: To increase coping skills to lessen anxiety<br><br>*Matthew*: To increase collaboration skills<br><br>*Rachel*: To increase independent study skills<br><br>*Ted*: To increase confidence<br><br>*Anthony*: To increase resiliency to stay with a task when challenging | *William*: Cars<br><br>*Matthew*: Drawing, dogs<br><br>*Rachel*: Animals, iPad, video games<br><br>*Ted*: Music, video games, baseball<br><br>*Anthony*: Sports, computer graphics |

**TABLE 2.2.** Class Learning Profile *(continued)*

| NETWORK | STUDENTS' STRENGTHS | STUDENTS' NEEDS | GENERAL STUDENTS' PREFERENCES/ INTERESTS |
|---|---|---|---|
| **Recognition** The ability to perceive presented information | *William*: Aware of his surroundings <br><br> *Matthew*: Strong background knowledge base <br><br> *Rachel*: Interprets visual charts, maps, graphs <br><br> *Ted*: Curious <br><br> *Anthony*: Attentive when information appears in color | *William*: To increase working memory <br><br> *Matthew*: To develop word decoding and fluency <br><br> *Rachel*: To increase word recognition <br><br> *Ted*: To increase independent inferencing skills when reading <br><br> *Anthony*: To increase word recognition, fluency, comprehension | |
| **Strategic** The ability to plan and follow through with an organized process of learning | *William*: Strong listening comprehension <br><br> *Matthew*: Organized <br><br> *Rachel*: Flexible and positive outlook <br><br> *Ted*: Identifies key words and strong summarizing skills <br><br> *Anthony*: Enjoys drawing, sketching, creating mind maps | *William*: To increase reading comprehension (fluency and vocabulary) and written expression (gathering information, organizing ideas, writing sentences, proofreading) <br><br> *Matthew*: To determine importance when locating key words, information <br><br> *Rachel*: To develop self-monitoring skills <br><br> *Ted*: To increase ability to transition from one idea/topic/activity to the next <br><br> *Anthony*: To increase independence when paraphrasing and identifying important information | |

Source: Rose & Meyer, 2002

Through a UDL lens, we acquire the knowledge that every learner has the ability to become an expert learner. That is, each learner has the ability to achieve to his or her personal absolute best. It is the decisions we educators make that provide the context for learning for all students to experience the process of becoming their best version of themselves as learners.

How do we do that? Let's return to the UDL Guidelines (see Figure 2.2). The top row outlines the ultimate goal for learners to achieve expert learner status. Ideally, expert learners are learners who are engaged, intrinsically motivated, and able to self-regulate. They are resourceful and knowledgeable and able to comprehend new information. Finally, expert learners are strategic and goal-directed, and are able to put successful executive functions firmly in place to allow them to plan, organize, and follow through with learning tasks to completion (CAST, 2011).

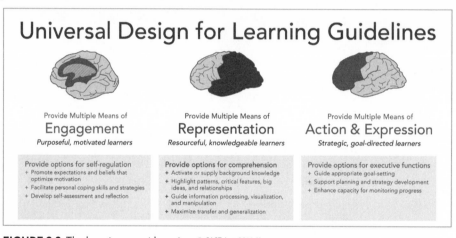

**FIGURE 2.2.** The keys to expert learning © CAST, Inc., 2014. Used with permission.

The middle and bottom row of the guidelines serve as checkpoints for us to create a positive journey toward each learner's right to become an expert learner. These two rows are checkpoints we can use to make sure we provide opportunities and scaffolds to guide each learner on his or her personal learning journey (see Figure 2.3).

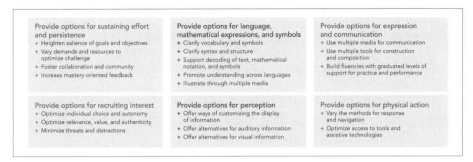

| Provide options for sustaining effort and persistence | Provide options for language, mathematical expressions, and symbols | Provide options for expression and communication |
|---|---|---|
| + Heighten salience of goals and objectives<br>+ Vary demands and resources to optimize challenge<br>+ Foster collaboration and community<br>+ Increase mastery-oriented feedback | + Clarify vocabulary and symbols<br>+ Clarify syntax and structure<br>+ Support decoding of text, mathematical notation, and symbols<br>+ Promote understanding across languages<br>+ Illustrate through multiple media | + Use multiple media for communication<br>+ Use multiple tools for construction and composition<br>+ Build fluencies with graduated levels of support for practice and performance |
| Provide options for recruiting interest | Provide options for perception | Provide options for physical action |
| + Optimize individual choice and autonomy<br>+ Optimize relevance, value, and authenticity<br>+ Minimize threats and distractions | + Offer ways of customizing the display of information<br>+ Offer alternatives for auditory information<br>+ Offer alternatives for visual information | + Vary the methods for response and navigation<br>+ Optimize access to tools and assistive technologies |

**FIGURE 2.3.** More keys to expert learning  © CAST, Inc., 2014. Used with permission.

## Another Tool: The Strength-based Inventory

In contrast with the concept of innate learning styles (see the sidebar "Why I Don't Talk about Learning Styles"), Thomas Armstrong (2012) draws on recent findings from neuroscience to emphasize the idea that skills and strengths develop and improve with practice. The brain physically changes as learning happens, and as it does, so does the capacity to learn in all sorts of ways. The findings from the science of neuroplasticity, or changeability, provide wonderful possibilities for us as teachers. We can view student variability as an opportunity to help students grow, rather than as a barrier we have to surmount. The implications for students in special education are tremendous. We can stop looking at students within the limited box that a classification label too often creates. We can acknowledge that each student has the capacity to grow and evolve as a flexible thinker who creates deeper learning experiences.

One tool to help guide us to get to know our students in an ongoing, meaningful way is the strengths-based approach (Armstrong, 2012). The strengths-based approach originated in the field of social work, where an emphasis on self-determination and the belief that every person has strengths to draw on are applied to the challenges facing particular clients. Armstrong adapts this to education. He recommends that in addition to gathering information from parents, previous teachers, cumulative files, and student inventories, we produce a strengths-based inventory for each student.

Inspired by Armstrong's 165-item strengths inventory, I created the following quick check-in tool (Figure 2.4) to not only guide the relationship-building between teachers and students but also to raise students' self-awareness of

Name_____    Date_____

## Check-In Reflection

1.  What is one personal strength that you feel proud of?

    _____
    _____
    _____

2.  Describe one way you are effective in communicating with others. For example, speaking, listening, writing, telling stories, telling jokes.

    _____
    _____
    _____

3.  What are your social strengths? For example, leadership abilities, helpful to others, socializing, show empathy for others.

    _____
    _____
    _____

4.  What are your emotional strengths? For example, positive attitude most of the time, able to push through struggles, accepts guidance from others, cares for other people.

    _____
    _____
    _____

5.  Name one intellectual strength that you notice. For example, musical, artistic, creative, math, science, nature, reading, writing.

    _____
    _____
    _____

6.  Name one physical strength that you notice. For example, exercise, bike riding, skateboarding, sports.

    _____
    _____
    _____

**FIGURE 2.4.** Quick survey to help learners build self-awareness

themselves as learners. This open-ended check-in can be used as a teacher-student interview, or teachers can ask students to complete it independently. I like to give this quick check-in once in September, and then ask students to complete the check-in again in March or April.

I recommend having students compare their two check-in reflections and see how they have evolved in their view about themselves over time. It can also serve as a powerful resource to guide students to create summer learning goals, or goals they would like to create for the upcoming school year. Respecting the presence of and providing opportunities for the unique minds (the neuro-diverse thinkers) that you have the privilege of working with each day is the foundation of UDL—and it is with this perspective that the value of learner variability is created and meaningful learning breathes through the classroom each day.

Again, the strengths-based inventory is just a tool that can open possibilities to more flexible education, not lock students into ideas of what they can or cannot accomplish. Learning will really take off in the co-taught classroom when both teachers recognize that every student has strengths, every student can learn, and every student can learn to learn—that is, to become an expert learner.

## PREPARING TO TEACH VARIABLE LEARNERS

Given the great range of abilities and diverse needs in the inclusive, co-taught classroom, UDL comes to the rescue with a framework that translates into a mind-set to guide us in creating meaningful learning experiences each day. Implementing the co-teaching models is just one layer of effective co-teaching. The co-teaching models alone just touch the surface of planning effective instruction. UDL is the next layer to designing instruction for the wide range of learner variability found in any inclusive classroom. Instructional decisions within the structure of selected co-teaching models must be accessible, relevant, and meaningful in order for learning to take place. The models help us to organize the structure of learning, and our belief in learner variability, along with the principles of UDL, provide the opportunities for us to address the wide range of learners found in our co-taught classrooms. UDL is all about solutions as we seek to connect each learner with deeper levels of learning.

An important part of the mission for all educators is to effectively navigate the swirling path between planning the curriculum (what they have to teach), implementing their instruction (how they will teach), and guiding their students' minds and hearts to become independent successful learners. Learning in any classroom comes with its own set of excitement and challenges. But additional challenges may easily be found in inclusive classroom settings. For example:

- How are the two teachers in the room going to balance and utilize each other's expertise in meaningful ways?

- How will the needs of a very diverse group of learners be met?

- How will the learners in the room be inspired to become ongoing learners who are self-motivated and independent thinkers?

- How will the two teachers make meaningful learning happen for their students and for themselves?

The answer to these and other challenging questions can be found within the framework of UDL. When the two teachers adopt a UDL mind-set that includes proactively planning, implementing, and assessing learning through a UDL lens, sparks fly—magic happens—everyone (including the two teachers!) continues to grow and learn in meaningful ways.

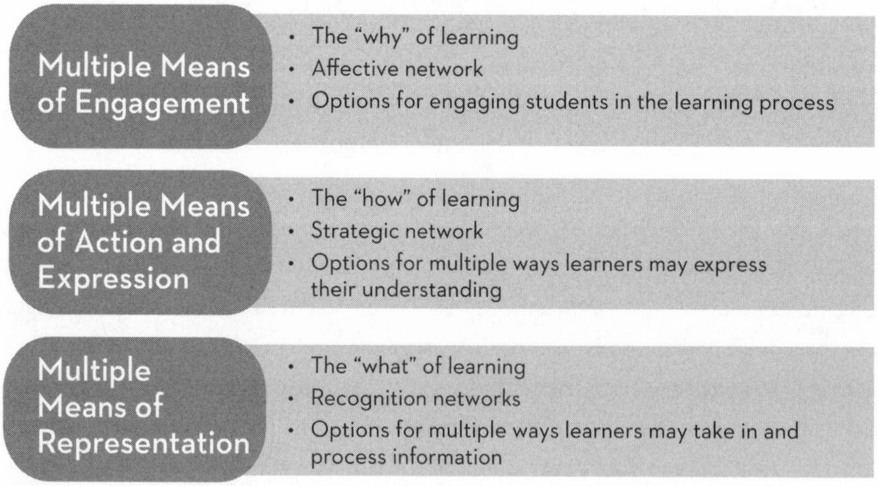

**Multiple Means of Engagement**
- The "why" of learning
- Affective network
- Options for engaging students in the learning process

**Multiple Means of Action and Expression**
- The "how" of learning
- Strategic network
- Options for multiple ways learners may express their understanding

**Multiple Means of Representation**
- The "what" of learning
- Recognition networks
- Options for multiple ways learners may take in and process information

**FIGURE 2.5.** The UDL principles and corresponding learning networks

The promise that UDL can elevate co-teaching through a view of learner variability blends seamlessly with the practice of providing high-powered instructional decisions as the planning and implementation phases. As mentioned earlier, engagement, representation, and action and expression are the three UDL principles that provide the opportunity for us to proactively plan for learner variability. These three principles transform our view of planning and implementing instruction into valuing each learner's unique abilities (and neuro-diversity) into viewing instruction through a UDL lens (Figure 2.5).

When UDL strategies are aligned with the learning networks and co-teaching models, instructional capability is expanded to reach all students, so each one has the ability to meaningfully connect to the content and the process of learning. In addition, the two teachers in the room will have the opportunity to share their personal expertise and be active participants in the instructional process. Table 2.3 shows how the learning networks, UDL Guidelines, and co-teaching models complement each other.

**TABLE 2.3.** Mapping Co-teaching Models to UDL and the Brain Networks

| BRAIN NETWORK | UDL GUIDELINES | EXAMPLE OF CO-TEACHING MODELS |
|---|---|---|
| **The Recognition Network**<br><br>Strategies that support the *what* of learning, so learners may recognize the information being taught | Provide multiple examples<br><br>Outline and highlight key information<br><br>Include options for recognition through multimedia and other formats | Station teaching or parallel teaching allows options for each teacher to present information in diverse ways—while keeping the same objective and high standards. |
| **The Strategic Network**<br><br>Strategies that support the learning process, so learners understand *how* to learn | Provide options for strategic thinking and organizing of information<br><br>Provide ongoing, immediate, and relevant feedback<br><br>Provide flexible opportunities to practice skills | Station teaching or parallel teaching allows for both teachers to provide options for strategic thinking and ongoing feedback.<br><br>The occasional, one-teach, one-assist, allows teachers to provide students with immediate, relevant feedback as one teacher focuses on instruction and the other teacher assesses and evaluates students' performance. |

**TABLE 2.3.** Mapping Co-teaching Models to UDL and the Brain Networks *(continued)*

| BRAIN NETWORK | UDL GUIDELINES | EXAMPLE OF CO-TEACHING MODELS |
|---|---|---|
| **The Strategic Network (continued)** | | Teaming can provide the option for one teacher to focus on the content while the other teacher focuses on the process of note-taking. The occasional alternative teaching can focus on one teacher pulling a small group to review a concept while teaching a specific strategy to guide learners' understanding. |
| **The Affective Network** Strategies that support engagement, so learners remain motivated and engaged throughout the learning process | Provide options for levels of thinking and levels of challenge Provide options for choice Offer various options for the context of learning Provide supports to guide learners to self-regulate and monitor their performance | Station teaching may enable teachers to provide choice to students, and provide time to guide self-monitoring and executive functioning skills. Teaming may provide the option for teachers to balance out the teaching of the content while ensuring the salience of high standards by supporting the process of thinking needed to master learning targets. |

All three networks and all UDL principles and Guidelines are well-supported within the natural framework of collaborative teaching and learning within all effective co-taught classrooms.

Let's take a look at what this means for our instructional decisions. When we consider that learners are variable in these three ways, we begin to design instruction in ways that take down any barriers to learning that may interfere between one or more students. Consider the co-teachers in this English class:

Joanne and Sophia are co-teaching (in any upper elementary or secondary classroom) an English lesson that requires learners to read closely to determine main ideas as well as to make logical inferences. Over the course of the week's lessons, students are asked to cite specific text evidence to support their thinking. Using the UDL principles, these teachers would be sure to do the following.

- Provide multiple ways to engage learners by:

  ▸ Creating a comfortable, risk-free feel to the environment

  ▸ Creating opportunities for students to process individually and then share their thinking with peers

  ▸ Highlighting the goals and learning objectives

  ▸ Incorporating personal strategies to guide learners to push through challenges

- Provide multiple means of representation by:

  ▸ Connecting the lesson to previously taught skills, strategies, and/or content (activate background knowledge)

  ▸ Highlighting, preteaching, offering vocabulary supports

  ▸ Providing multimedia options such as visual aids, use of digital technology, auditory supplements

- Provide multiple means of action and expression by:

  ▸ Offering options for ways students express their thinking—allowing for creative ways to express thinking based on your specific learning goal. For example, when locating text evidence, students may speak, write, or underline/highlight.

  ▸ Offering options for access to resources and tools. For example, some students may experience the process of reading on paper, others on a digital version on an iPad, and others may listen by having someone read aloud or by listening to a digital audio version.

  ▸ Exposing students to strategies to guide their personal learning strengths and needs. The strategies should guide them for this lesson, but also be strengthening their reading skills in general.

As we gain a deeper understanding of UDL, we must use our initial awareness of the UDL principles to embrace learner variability. We must move our awareness and desire to meet the needs of variable learners into the practice of our instructional decisions.

# TAKEAWAY IDEAS

- All classrooms are filled with variable learners. Disability is just one aspect of variability. However, in inclusive, co-taught classrooms, the range of variability may put more demands on the teachers in terms of preparation and execution.

- The co-teaching models alone are not enough to support teachers' needs, but the UDL principles and guidelines can be used to help co-teachers anticipate and lower any potential instructional barriers so that each learner can succeed.

- Both teachers must be valued as active participants with expertise to share in the instructional process.

# STUDY GROUP QUESTIONS

1. What does variability mean to you? How does your view of variability inform your instructional process?

2. Align the three UDL principles with what you learned about the three brain networks. How does your understanding connect to your current teaching style?

3. Think of one or two recent lessons and share how the three brain networks and UDL principles were naturally embedded. What were specific teaching moves and/or strategies that highlighted specific UDL principles?

4. Why do you think the three brain networks, the UDL Guidelines, and the co-teaching models align so naturally to deepen the learning experiences for everyone in the room?

# Instructional Design: Making the UDL Mind-set Shift

# 3

HOPEFULLY BY THIS POINT, YOU ARE BEGINNING TO SEE HOW UDL CAN ELEVATE INSTRUCTION IN THE CO-TAUGHT CLASSROOM. For those not yet convinced, take all the time you need. The concepts and framework of UDL run contrary to much of what we've learned as teachers. Adopting UDL requires a shift in our mind-sets as much as it does a shift in our strategies and tactics. You want to do all you can for *each* student in your classroom; that desire will help as you work to understand and apply these powerful ideas. So let's continue to dig deeper into understanding UDL by seeing how it applies to instructional design and planning.

UDL is based on a wide range of research in education practices, cognitive psychology, and neuroscience. Through extensive research we know about how people learn, what motivates learners, and how to engage them in a process of self-regulated learning that results in independent, successful learners. When planned proactively and implemented with flexibility, UDL-based lessons give learners opportunities to enter the learning process through many entry points of understanding. So, for example, if one student has difficulty reading grade-level texts, scaffolds are built into the instruction that offer options for students to engage in the learning.

There is no such thing as "can't" in the UDL classroom. It is a knock-down-all-barriers approach that supports all students in achieving their personal best. And along this path, learners focus on their strengths while working to compensate for any apparent areas of weakness. Let's face it: All learners have a blend of both, so why not guide students to use their strengths to compensate or strengthen their areas of weakness? Going back to our student who is reading below grade level, why not use his strength in receptive language and provide audio books or online tools to provide text-to-speech supports?

So often, we as educators reflexively follow the traditional deficit model when viewing learners. We look at the bell curve and see where students fall in regard to certain skills. We are forced to see their weaknesses, and then our educational focus becomes misdirected and we try to "fix" the weaknesses. We become educator zombies who race the clock as we try to keep our students up to date with the fast-paced curriculum expectations. Along the way, students' self-esteem, hope, and energy sink lower and lower as experience after experience, grade after grade, force this negative view of themselves as learners. In addition, well-intentioned teachers become part of this deficit-model frenzy where students' personal gaps may be closing a bit each year, but the gap remains because these students are now in the next grade—and still one, two, or more years behind grade-level expectations.

# BREAKING THROUGH THE DEFICIT-MODEL BARRIER

Our current view of students with disabilities does not help our mission to value and educate all learners. In fact, this current view is undoubtedly one strong barrier to creating inclusive settings. To qualify for special education, a student's strengths and needs are evaluated and his or her performance is perceived along the all-too-familiar bell curve where we can see how close to the "average range" the student falls. If the student's standard score places her between 85 and 115, she is considered to be performing within the average range. The closer to 100 that the student performs, the closer to average she is considered. Students who perform below the range of accepted norms are considered to exhibit weaknesses that may need to be addressed through special education services. If the student qualifies for special education, she must meet the criteria for eligibility for one of the 13 categories of special education as defined by the Individuals with Disabilities Education Act (IDEA):

- Autism

- Blindness

- Deafness

- Emotional Disturbance

- Hearing Impairment

- Intellectual Disability

- Multiple Disabilities

- Orthopedic Impairment

- Other Health Impaired

- Specific Learning Disability

- Speech or Language Impairment

- Traumatic Brain Injury

- Visual Impairment

Our current system of special education encourages us to view students' abilities through this deficit model. We evaluate the student's abilities with a zoom lens pointing to what he cannot do as compared to typically developing peers. We decide what educational placements, programs, and strategies need to be in place to support this student's areas of weakness.

This view of a students' deficits predisposes them to the cloud of being negatively labeled as students with disabilities. This cloud accentuates what they cannot do—and what we, as educators, must do to help them. The way our educational system and society view these classifications far too often creates a barrier to learning. Learners easily develop a narrow view of themselves as learners—simply by the messages (both direct and indirect) that parents, educators, and community members share. This deficit model becomes a way of thinking that focuses on the students' disabilities rather than the students' abilities.

However, when we as educators view learners through a UDL lens, we consider all students as variable learners. We accept the strengths and needs of students as an authentic group of learners who are individual thinkers. Students' strengths and needs are proactively considered in ways that positively address learning needs—and by doing so, we can help guide them to reach their absolute personal best.

Making the shift from a deficit mind-set to a UDL mind-set will open a world of learning to students and educators. As you read the pages of this book, you will continue to gain the knowledge, insights, and skills needed to make UDL a natural mind-set for educators. I have found that keeping a focus on UDL knocks down the attitudinal barriers created by viewing a learner through his deficits. With UDL, I know I am doing what is in each student's best interest—with the hope of creating students who understand how their personal learning strengths can become the access point for successful learning. The idea is for educators to instill the knowledge and experiences of a meaningful process of learning—not just have learners experience the assign-and-assess mode where the only thing they remember is a grade, a product, or some meaningless end result.

Learning in a UDL classroom is a process. What we expect is that students will learn to take that process outside the classroom, to become independent in connecting their environment and experiences with the content. The classroom is the place to plant the seeds of motivation, where students are engaged and eager to learn through a challenging, memorable, and rewarding process. Now that we have a foundation for understanding how to elevate instruction through the co-teaching models with a UDL mind-set, we can begin to approach the tough questions:

- What do we do for learners who require more supports and scaffolds?

- How do we truly include each learner in our planning and implementation of meaningful learning experiences?

- How do we plan and design instruction that removes barriers so students are now able to create personal connections and meaning with the content and materials?

We can be confident that if UDL strategies are embedded in the learning process, all learners, including students with special needs, will meet with success and gain the ability to become more independent learners. Once UDL scaffolds and the use of co-teaching models have removed as many barriers as possible, the co-teachers' minds and time are more focused on recognizing what additional scaffolds and support are needed by students with more intensive needs. We have now created a learning environment where all learners—including those with more intensive needs—have the opportunity to become expert learners.

As inclusive settings become a natural part of the options for educating students with disabilities, we must make sure that special education teachers advocate well for their expertise as strategic, process-oriented educators. A special education teacher's training includes setting goals, monitoring goals, and scaffolding support to guide students toward independence. As standards-based expectations rise for all students, special education teachers must make sure to insert strategic supports within the moments of the general education instructional setting.

Enter *specially designed instruction (SDI)*.

## BLENDING SPECIALLY DESIGNED INSTRUCTION AND UDL PLANNING

SDI is what special education teachers are trained to do—to create specialized instruction to meet the needs of particular learners. SDI is the thoughtful process of designing instruction by adapting the content, methodology, or delivery of instruction to accommodate a learner's disability. These adaptations ensure access to the general education curriculum so that learners may work toward learning goals and expectations as outlined by the student's Individualized Education Plan (IEP), district expectations, and the core standards adopted by the state.

SDI is a planned, organized, and meaningful process that is intentional and systematic and addresses the student's needs as expressed in the student's IEP. This specialized focus must link with the general education curriculum and learning targets. It is part of the special education teacher's responsibility to make sure that SDI is a natural part of the learning environment in a co-taught classroom. SDI is part of the logical and legal process of making sure that a student's IEP and individualized needs are being met. SDI is what makes the role of the special education teacher in the inclusive setting valuable and necessary. There will be students who need more supports beyond what the universal scaffolds offer.

Let's consider two co-teachers who are creating an accessible learning environment for learners to read, comprehend, and express their understanding. Let's add a focus to three students in that class who have weak decoding, comprehension, writing, and organization skills.

The scaffolds in place through the co-teaching models and UDL strategies serve to remove important barriers. For example, having the text read to them through options of multimedia and teacher supports guide and engage the students' comprehension skills. The options for expressing their comprehension through writing are supported by allowing them to sketch and speak in peer collaborations. Yet students with more intensive needs require further supports—and this is the purpose of the inclusive setting.

One of the main purposes of having a special education teacher in the room is so that SDI will be a natural part of the learning process and so that further supports and interventions will be included beyond the UDL scaffolds that help all learners. So let's put this together:

- Co-teaching models provide the structure to organize learning, but these models alone do not create meaningful learning. These models are the outer shell that supports the potential for powerful learning to occur.

- UDL principles, guidelines, and strategies provide educators with options for elevating instruction. They are the strategies and scaffolds that create a clear, meaningful pathway, so that all learners can connect within the moments of instructional time.

- Specially designed instruction must come into play when co-teachers are designing instruction and planning for those students who require further supports and interventions as outlined in their IEPs. SDI must be evident in all co-taught classrooms. If it is not present, then why have the special education teacher assigned to the class in the first place?

Continuing with our example, as we focus on the three students who need additional supports, the co-teachers must make time to provide explicit instruction in decoding, comprehension, writing, and organization. This can be done within the structure of this lesson. Since the students are in small groups, teachers may have the flexibility to work more explicitly with some students. In addition, these teachers must be mindful to incorporate these strategic and explicit supports on a regular basis. A UDL mind-set and the co-teaching models create this flexibility and lower the number of barriers that these students have to contend with during any given lesson. In addition, ongoing communication between the general education and special education teacher will ensure a smooth flow to the process of learning.

# POWERING UP WITH THE UDL GUIDELINES

So far we have discussed the value of implementing a variety of co-teaching models to structure the learning in an inclusive, co-taught classroom. In addition, embracing a UDL mind-set is the next layer to ensuring that the instruction within the selected co-teaching models is designed to create access and meaningful learning for each learner.

## ▶ Differentiated Instruction and UDL

*Differentiated instruction* (*DI*; Tomlinson, 1999) is one of the techniques frequently applied within the process of effective SDI. Differentiation is also a natural part of the UDL process. Educators know that in order to make learning meaningful, students must attach personal connections to ensure motivation and retention. Therefore, educators must consider students' needs, interests, and abilities. Tomlinson (1999) suggests that in order to create effective classroom environments, teachers must differentiate lessons and activities to support learners' various interests, learning profiles and levels of readiness. Teachers accommodate and make instructional decisions that support individual student needs. Students are provided with choices to make the learning process authentic and meaningful to each learner in the room.

In a UDL classroom, differentiating instruction is embedded into the planning, implementation, and assessment. All too often teachers become overwhelmed at the mere thought of differentiating instruction. The pacing of instruction, coupled with the varying levels of students' abilities, often results in a teacher claiming he does not have time to differentiate. Yet there is a way to make differentiating instruction a natural part of the planning and learning process.

When we approach the idea of differentiating instruction, we will be successful if we look through a UDL lens. When teachers apply differentiation without a UDL perspective, the focus tends to be on "fixing the learner." These teachers go about trying to fit in strategies to support specific deficits in a student's learning profile. For example, if Gregory has a weakness in decoding, the teachers may support him by saying, "How can we make it so Gregory can decode this text? How can we increase his decoding ability, so he can learn alongside his peers?"

Here the focus is on Gregory's weakness and the teachers' valiant efforts to erase the weakness. Yet frustration ensues because the pacing of the curriculum along with the level of complexity of the text just keeps a one- to two-year achievement gap in place as he continues the grades.

A teacher who differentiates instruction through a UDL lens takes a proactive approach to lowering barriers for all learners from the outset. The emphasis is on "fixing" the curriculum in order to make it more flexible and accessible. Considering the case of Gregory, as the teachers provide UDL scaffolds for all learners by including multimedia text-to-speech along with teacher- and peer-supported opportunities, the barriers that Gregory might face are anticipated and addressed before instruction even begins. Just-in-time supports are already available. More explicit decoding instruction (keeping SDI in mind) during other points in the day may be necessary to supplement these proactive strategies. But differentiating alone may create a learning environment where teachers categorize their students through their learning style preferences that often do not fit within the context of learning for a particular lesson. When differentiating alone, teachers may easily end up reteaching because in the moments of class time, the focus was on having the students fit into a rigid curriculum. From a UDL perspective, the focus is on having the curriculum fit into the various needs of all learners. The needs of all students are met through natural scaffolds and opportunities for them to take charge of their own learning.

**TABLE 3.1:** UDL and DI at a glance

| UDL | DI |
|---|---|
| Is **proactive** in considering multiple pathways for learning and communicating through student choice. | Oftentimes **reactive** because the teacher plans for learning style options, yet the options may be too rigid and misaligned with students' learning style strengths for the context of that lesson. |
| The focus is on "fixing" the curriculum, so that all students may easily participate, learn, and express their learning in ways that make sense to them. | The focus is on "fixing" the learner. Teachers start with their lesson plan and say, "How can I help this learner achieve this lesson's goals?" Learning style options are often provided, but the aim is toward fitting the learner into a rigid goal or end product expectation. |

When applying UDL, all students have options to perceive, apply strategies, and express their understanding in ways that deepen their personal learning experiences. Learning preferences may change from lesson to lesson depending on the context. High expectations are set for all learners, and the process to achieve those high expectations is supported through natural scaffolds that work to guide learners to connect personally to the curriculum. In order for powerful learning environment to unfold, the co-teachers must develop a positive co-teaching relationship.

But what happens with those students who need more support? These are the variable learners in our room with IEPs who require more explicit instruction with additional supports. As we have discussed, UDL is a way to design instruction to make sure that any unintentional instructional and learning barriers are taken away from the beginning. When UDL is considered, teachers create a more accessible learning environment that increases the opportunities for learners to meaningfully interact with the material, participate in the process of learning, and gain personal academic and social skills that lead to deeper understandings.

For example, let's consider this scenario. The learning goal in this inclusive classroom requires students to demonstrate their comprehension of a text by writing a summary paragraph. Through the UDL lens, the co-teachers consider that the skills require students to demonstrate decoding, fluency, comprehension, knowledge of vocabulary, and written expression. The teachers know they have students who struggle with these tasks. The teachers then consider the co-teaching models and decide which structure(s) would help to create access. They look at the UDL Guidelines to guide the types of scaffolds they could provide for specific student needs. They also know they do not have a lot of time to prepare this lesson.

Here's how it could play out:

**Considering multiple means of engagement,** the teachers decide to increase student interest by providing choices. They offer three options for a first reading of the text. The students may read the text silently, they may listen to the text using headphones and visual and audio supports on Chromebooks, or they may choose to read the text in a shared reading group with one of the teachers.

**Considering multiple means of representation,** the teachers explore options for perception by providing a vocabulary list written on chart paper with definitions, as well as vocabulary supports through use of a dictionary/thesaurus app. The text will be offered via multimedia through Chromebooks. Teachers will facilitate comprehension by providing feedback, modeling the process of visualization through a think-aloud approach, and modeling decoding and fluency.

**Considering multiple means of action and expression,** the teachers decide to vary their methods of response. They know that, eventually, each student must provide a written summary paragraph. However, they know that a few students need some scaffolding to support the organization of their thoughts. The teachers again decide to allow students to illustrate their ideas by sketching key concepts and then writing a descriptive caption of their sketch(es). (This will be used to support their writing of the paragraph in the near future.) Students also have the option to work with a peer, where one peer will speak and the other peer will write what the other has said. The peers then switch roles, so that both students have the opportunity to speak and write—yet it is a collaborative process that guides deeper understandings.

Both teachers are happy with the ideas for supporting students' skill sets. They decide that a team teaching–co-teaching model will be best for opening the lesson. They then move to student choice groups (a modified version of station teaching) and provide one-to-one assistance and small-group instruction, as needed. During the opening of the lesson and team teaching approach, one teacher engages the class in a review of active reading strategies. The other teacher takes over by previewing the vocabulary words through class discussion and use of the visual chart. Both teachers add their thoughts along the way. It is a quick 15-minute opening that creates the support, structure, and engagement for each learner in the room to connect with the lesson.

It was a lesson that did not take a lot of time to plan and prepare—the co-teaching models and the UDL scaffolds were naturally embedded in a way to focus on the learning goals. The UDL scaffolds, along with the structure of their specifically selected co-teaching models, "fixed" the curriculum by providing an accessible process of learning for each student. Students with and without IEPs were given the supports they needed to meaningfully participate in the learning.

Creating lessons and units for any classroom becomes a positive experience with a UDL mind-set. However, there is additional value and necessity to apply the process of UDL with inclusive classrooms where learner variability clearly spans a wide spectrum of abilities. Educators fall into natural planning and instructional routines where they proactively plan in ways that consider how the three UDL principles align with students' needs and ability to connect to material. In addition, a UDL mind-set becomes natural in the moments of instruction because teachers are flexible in meeting the needs of students during the actual learning moments.

For example, consider a teacher who plans for students to gain important social studies content through the use of visuals such as a SMART Board presentation and whole-class discussion. As the lesson unfolds, she realizes that this visual modality is not enough. She makes a decision within the moments of the lesson to allow for students to further investigate the material through cooperative learning discussions and use of iPads so that students can explore the topic through their own research. Using proactive planning and additional learning pathways helps this teacher plan for realistic learner variability rather than singling out (or even worse, ignoring!) those students in the margins.

I shudder to think for a moment about the teacher who muddles through the SMART Board lesson with the whole-class discussion where students' learning needs are not met. What happens next? Well, we know the story. . .students become disengaged and disenchanted, and over time do not demonstrate their true capabilities as learners. Educators with a UDL mind-set believe that students achieve their personal best when lessons are proactively planned for all learners in mind. Let's erase the margins and create true inclusive settings!

So how do we get the content, high expectations, learning targets, skills, and strategies across to our students? We know it's not simply a matter of providing the lecture or the visuals and, voilà, students have gained all the knowledge and skills we intended to teach. Effective teaching is much deeper than that. Scaffolding the instruction is the golden ticket that teachers can provide to students in the inclusive classroom. It is their opportunity to become active learners who gain knowledge, skills, and strategies through learning processes. When taught well, these strategies will become a part of the student's repertoire of learning tools to guide him to be an independent learner. In one of his famous talks on teaching and creativity, Sir Ken Robinson states that teaching is an art form. His words make me feel like he is right here in the conversation with us:

> That's why I always say that teaching is an art form. It's not a delivery system. I don't know when we started confusing teaching with FedEx. Teaching is an arts practice. It's about connoisseurship and judgment and intuition. We all remember the great teachers in our lives. The ones who kind of woke us up and that we're still thinking about because they said something to us or they gave us an angle on something that we've never forgotten. (Robinson, 2014)

## SCAFFOLDS, SCAFFOLDS, SCAFFOLDS

The scaffolds we create become the tools of our artistic creations. In the UDL classroom, teachers create learning environments where a student's classifications are not used as a way of defining who she is as a learner. When teachers create UDL environments, all students value their thinking and their learning process, and embrace the process it takes to gain and retain knowledge. As we mentioned earlier, the UDL Guidelines provide specific ideas for naturally incorporating strategies to scaffold students' learning to make the process as meaningful as possible.

We have early 20th century Russian psychologist Lev Vygotsky to thank for the concept of scaffolding the learning for our students. In fact, Vygotsky's work (1978) naturally supports CAST's framework for the three brain networks (recognition, strategic, and affective systems) that we discussed earlier in this chapter. Vygotsky suggested through his research that each learner has a zone of proximal development (ZPD)—that is, the sweet spot where learners are challenged and, with a little support, can learn even more. At the lower level of the zone, learners can reach certain levels on their own; with additional assistance, they can achieve challenging tasks without getting too frustrated. When assistance is provided with the appropriate level of scaffolds, learners could become independent and reach higher levels of thinking and performance. Those scaffolds can then be gradually released as learners grow in skill or knowledge. It is within that opportunity for learning with assistance and scaffolds that learners push beyond limitations or barriers. These learning opportunities begin by educators recognizing the present levels of performance (the learner's zone of actual development) and then scaffolding the learning to guide deeper learning and greater independence in time (Vygotsky, 1986).

Learners are active within a process of learning toward independence. Within a cycle of instruction, students are engaged along a series of steps that begins with an explicit modeling by the teacher(s) to provide full disclosure of how to apply a particular skill or strategy. The teacher then engages in a relaxed "let's try this together" mind-set, so students have the opportunity to begin to apply a skill or strategy, but with guidance, as needed. Once the interactive "we do" phase is completed, the students are directed to practice on their own. The teacher(s) may provide options for students to work in pairs, in groups, or individually. The teacher(s) use this time to monitor students' progress and to guide independent application. Figure 3.1 illustrates this model.

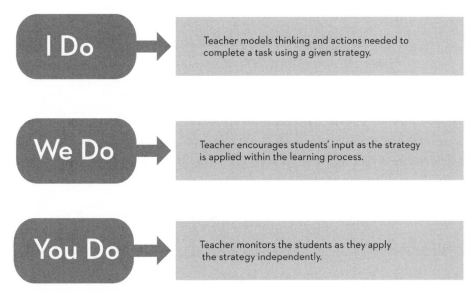

**FIGURE 3.1.** Scaffolding learners' independence

The scaffolded structure in Figure 3.1 provides the right balance of teacher support and student application. The learning process is naturally embedded with the right degree of challenge to keep students eager to apply their knowledge and skills on their way to becoming resourceful, strategic learners. When students are engaged in meaningful and challenging work, motivation to learn increases (Gargiulo & Metcalf, 2013). This workshop model will be discussed again in Chapter 5, "UDL in Action." As we continue on our journey of connecting co-teaching with a UDL mind-set, it is important to gain a deeper sense of the foundation for designing instruction with meaningful scaffolding.

# KEEPING EXPECTATIONS HIGH FOR EVERY LEARNER

We have talked about the need to truly believe that every student can learn, and that it is our responsibility to provide the learning environment that makes that possible. Throughout history, students with disabilities were given less complex tasks or were given accommodations that modified the curriculum in ways that expected them to do less. Through neuroscience and educational research, we know that the variability of all learners can be supported through instruction that is strong with scaffolds to guide students to connect meaningfully with the content.

Renowned special education researcher Edwin Ellis (1999) talks of "watering up the curriculum"—that is, offering the scaffolds, supports, and accommodations that maintain high expectations for all learners rather than dumbing down the curriculum. In the following paragraphs, I take nine goals outlined by Ellis (1999) and show how they can provide additional checkpoints for teachers as they weave high expectations with UDL supports into their learning environments. Ellis's nine goals connect seamlessly to the UDL principles and guidelines.

1.  **More emphasis on students constructing knowledge**

    Teachers facilitate learning to allow students to seek information, process it, and express their understandings. Students have opportunities to connect previously learned information with new information.

    **The UDL Connection:**

    Consider multiple means of action and expression. Offer multiple tools and strategy to use. Vary the methods of response to allow each learner to connect and express her expanded knowledge in meaningful ways.

2.  **More depth, less superficial coverage**

    Teachers deliver learning experiences that allow students to process ideas and understand why they are important and how they connect. Teachers make time to experience learning with students rather than just covering the information based on what is written in their plan book or curriculum guide.

The UDL Connection:

Consider multiple means of representation to allow students to perceive information in welcoming, familiar, and exciting ways. Once students make that first meaningful step, move the lesson into an active process where they are actively thinking, speaking, sharing, and learning.

3. More emphasis on developing relational understanding and knowledge connections

As a way to guide deeper understandings, teachers provide students with the opportunity to see how ideas and concepts are connected. Information is taught within a context of what a student knows to allow him to associate new learning with known information.

The UDL Connection:

Consider multiple means of engagement. How can you optimize relevance, value, and authenticity as you connect your goals, content, and materials with the strengths and needs of your students? Be a keen observer, so you may read and understand how to guide each learner. Guide learners through multiple means of action and expression to connect new learning with previously taught information.

4. More student elaboration

Include many opportunities for students to not only hear their own thoughts but also share their voice. Cooperative learning, such as think-pair-share, provides valuable processing time for students to gain deeper understandings as well as confidence in their abilities.

The UDL Connection:

Consider multiple means of action and expression as you support strategy development.

5. **More emphasis on the redundancy of archetype concepts, patterns, and strategies**

   Teachers facilitate learning in ways that guide learners to see connections, repetition, and associations to guide their understanding and memory for important information. For example, students are taught themes of geography to guide their understanding when learning about ancient civilizations.

   The UDL Connection:

   Consider multiple means of representation as you introduce new ideas. Including visuals and multimedia options through multiple means of action and expression will get students to see and experience the connections and associations to guide deeper understanding and retention.

6. **More reflection and risk-taking**

   Teachers incorporate time for students to think about how they feel about what they are learning. They experiment with strategies that guide their learning, and they are free to share their ideas within an environment where their thinking is valued.

   The UDL Connection:

   Consider multiple means of engagement to foster a collaborative learning community where students reflect and self-regulate the application of specific strategies.

7. **More social support for achievement**

   Create opportunities for learners to strengthen their own voice as they develop tolerance and understanding for the views of others. In inclusive classrooms, cooperative learning and peer interactions are ideal opportunities for all learners to take the lead in learning, as well as learn from their peers.

   The UDL Connection:

   Consider multiple means of engagement as you nurture an environment where learners value their thinking and are comfortable sharing their voice with peers. As students share their views, they learn to value the perspective of their peers.

8. More emphasis on developing habits of mind, thinking skills, and learning strategies

Learners have ongoing opportunities to develop a growth mind-set as they push through challenges. In addition, they learn a variety of strategies to guide them to be successful.

The UDL Connection:

Consider multiple means of action and expression, along with engagement, as learners set goals, plan, and apply strategies that optimize learning and self-reflection.

9. More emphasis on developing a sense of personal potency

The individual thinking of variable learners is valued. Each learner is supported along a learning process that fosters interpersonal, intrapersonal, and academic success.

The UDL Connection:

Consider all three UDL principles. Multiple means of engagement will connect learners with goals and self-reflection. Multiple means of representation will allow each learner to maximize personal connections and transfer of material. Multiple means of action and expression will support strategic, goal-directed learners.

The better learners connect the content with their own background knowledge, the more they will learn and remember. Research shows that when instruction is rigorous and allows each learner to have the opportunity to connect meaningfully with the learning, he will meet with new levels of personal success. And that is our overall mission of UDL—to create expert learners.

# TAKEAWAY IDEAS

Weaving UDL within the instructional process while varying the application of co-teaching models is a way to reach the different learners that make up any inclusive setting.

- UDL is a proactive process that creates a powerful mind-set and guides educators to design classroom instruction that connects all students to a meaningful learning process within the moments of instruction.

- UDL naturally includes all learners and embraces the value of learner voice and learner strengths, while supporting them to learn more, to do more, and to become more. Differentiating instruction is considered a proactive focus that removes barriers within the instruction and the curriculum.

- When differentiation is applied without a UDL lens, the focus is on "fixing" the learner—which is why it can feel like a daunting task. When differentiation is applied through a UDL lens, the focus is on "fixing" the curriculum (not on "fixing" the student). The instruction is designed with scaffolds in place to support the natural variability of all learners.

- UDL fosters personal and academic growth as each learner experiences the effects of becoming an expert learner (achieving her absolute personal best). Variable teaching styles and areas of teacher expertise are applied through the co-teaching models and through strategic best practice.

- Designing instruction with UDL strategies removes many instructional barriers and creates an accessible learning environment with opportunities for meaningful deeper learning activities. Some students in an inclusive classroom will require further supports through the special education teacher's expertise and application of specially designed instruction.

- Co-plan to implement UDL strategies for all students by providing scaffolds and strategies to support the three brain networks, and make sure to add specially designed instructional strategies to further support students who require additional scaffolds.

# STUDY GROUP QUESTIONS

1. How do you and your co-teacher(s) view your students? Is your focus on "fixing" the learners or "fixing" the curriculum to remove instructional barriers? Share an example.

2. On a scale of O to 5, where 5 is the most positive, how do you rate yourself in terms of embracing learner variability? How often to you fall into the deficit-model trap? What can you do to wholeheartedly embrace the view of learner variability? Where does your co-teacher stand? How can you both come together to make learner variability a natural belief and mind-set for all learners in your room?

3. What is the value of scaffolding in the instructional process? Share one or two examples of how your instructional scaffolds guided learners in your classroom to meet with great success.

4. What are some barriers that exist within your instructional process? Think about your planning, implementing, and assessment practices.

5. What are some ways that you encourage students to take charge of their learning? What are the specific scaffolds that you build into the learning process?

# PART
# 2

# Teacher Workshop: Elevating Co-teaching by Applying UDL

# 4

# Planning Powerful Instruction

THE ULTIMATE PURPOSE FOR PLANNING EFFECTIVE INSTRUCTION IS FOR STUDENT ACHIEVEMENT. We as educators strive to increase students' broad knowledge base and guide them to strengthen the skills that all learners need to become successful lifelong learners. Teachers are facilitators within a process that nurtures learners as they reach new heights and depths of their personal best. It is through the curriculum that we are able to reach each student. Curriculum is what we plan to teach, how we plan to teach it, and knowing when we have accomplished our learning targets with our students. Joshua Hendrickson, LMSW— a social-and-emotional-learning consultant and the executive director of Project Presence—has guided me to hold curriculum as a living, breathing experience shared between teacher and student.

So first things first. . .

The essence of the UDL framework makes it possible for teachers to address individual differences in our students' affective, recognition, and strategic networks. Through proactive decisions and flexible thinking within the moments of instruction, teachers can support variable learners by individualizing pathways to learning.

- Flexible methods and materials—the heart of UDL implementation—create the opportunity for learning to be a personal, meaningful experience for all learners in the room (including the teachers!).

- Specified, clear learning goals are set and each student has the opportunity to achieve at his personal best through clearly planned pathways for heightened engagement and successful outcomes (Rose & Meyer, 2002).

- Assessment is woven through the learning process. Formative ongoing assessments provide meaningful information about how each student is learning in real time, with the focus on the process and performance—information teachers need to guide their instructional decisions.

Through the four components of a UDL curriculum, the planning, implementation, and assessment process becomes clear and focused. The curriculum provides us with a deeper understanding that we are in control of what happens in our classrooms. The focus for providing multiple pathways to learning starts to take shape and we begin to apply the value and urgency of making meaningful instructional decisions each day.

With UDL, it is very easy to create the curriculum as a living, breathing experience between teachers and students (see Figure 4.1).

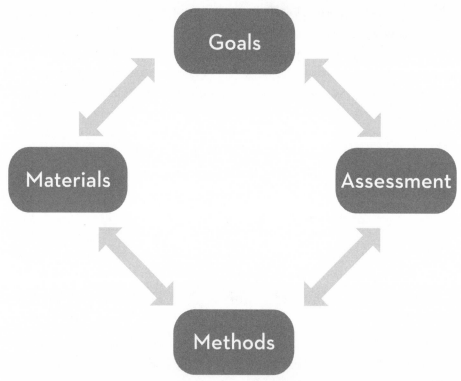

**FIGURE 4.1.** Four components of curriculum (per Rose & Meyer, 2002)

The instructional cycle in a UDL classroom blends the four components of curriculum with learners' abilities to build knowledge (recognition networks), build strategies and skills (strategic networks), and build the stamina and persistence needed for learning (affective networks). As co-teachers design the instructional process through a UDL lens, they create a masterful flow of meaningful learning opportunities for each student.

# CONTRASTING TRADITIONAL AND UDL APPROACHES TO CURRICULUM

A great way to understand UDL is to contrast traditional and UDL approaches to the four components of curriculum: goals, materials, methods, and assessment (Sabia, 2008). I've found this to be a helpful tool in my own practice. Let's try it here.

## Goals

Traditional instructional goals express what the students will be able to accomplish. For example, *students will read the nonfiction article on the water cycle and write a one-paragraph summary of the key points and orally present their summary to the class.* When goals are stated this way, some students in the class will not be able to achieve this goal.

A UDL goal leaves the means to achievement open-ended. For example, *students will learn key facts about the water cycle and will demonstrate their mastery of this information by selecting one of the expression options.* Writing the goal in this way lets students personally connect to the content and provides an opportunity for them to demonstrate what they have learned in a manner that guides meaningful learning. Students will be given options for representation to address possible barriers of decoding, or they may choose to use online sources with a text-to-speech program that allows them to hear the text read aloud. If oral expression presents a barrier for a student due to a disability or anxiety, the student may use other ways to demonstrate mastery, such as creating a PowerPoint or a Prezi presentation.

It is important to distinguish between instructional goals and Individualized Education Plan (IEP) goals. Instructional goals focus on achieving the necessary grade-level content. IEP goals refer to the individualized goals set for the student to guide her to strengthen the skills needed to extend her content knowledge. IEP and instructional goals are easily aligned and should always guide the learner to strengthen individualized skills while learning content knowledge. For example, incorporating cooperative learning activities where all students have the opportunity to share their thinking around content knowledge could address an IEP goal of increasing a particular student's ability to work with peers and collaborate. Another example: Having all students complete a note-taking organizer to help gather particular content could simultaneously meet an IEP goal that addresses a particular student's need to increase organization, note-taking, and/or study skills.

Notice that by creating a goal through this UDL lens, we stay focused on what we are teaching rather than focused on one fixed way we want students to learn it. Through this UDL perspective, we create a clear path between the content, the strategies, and affective learning processes.

## Instructional Materials

It doesn't take much effort to think about what the traditional curriculum materials look like. Unfortunately, having desks that form rows of learners facing the front of the room with their textbooks, worksheets, or workbooks on their desks is a view that quickly comes into mind. This image can be shattered as we allow UDL to broaden our opportunities and our integration of materials by using digital versions of printed materials, videos, graphic novels, dry-erase boards, musical instruments, and any other multimedia that provides options for multiple means of accessing, expressing, and assessing understanding through the learning process.

For example, varied font size and background color can be used to enhance visual presentation. Sections of a text can be reformatted to meet specific students' needs. For example, consider reformatting printed material by chunking sections of reading and providing wider margins and space between paragraphs. That way, students can monitor their comprehension in sections to achieve better organization and comprehension. This option addresses the instructional goal of gaining content knowledge, as well as an IEP goal that specifies a student's ability to self-monitor and increase his comprehension of grade-level texts. Text-to-speech features can be used to support students with decoding and comprehension needs.

As UDL parent-advocate and lecturer Ricki Sabia (2008) notes:

An increased use of digital materials will require a paradigm shift in terms of how technology is used in most schools so that more technology is brought into the classroom. This is the perfect time for such a shift since most districts are developing technology initiatives to prepare students for employment in the 21st century. (pp. 15–16)

Teachers who view the materials through a UDL lens believe that all learners in their classroom use the materials to deepen their personal understandings and to demonstrate their knowledge. Materials must be purposeful and meaningful to each learner in the class throughout the learning process.

## Methods

Think about the first thing that comes to mind when you imagine the learning process in any classroom. For some, lecture-style presentations where the teacher is the "sage on stage" came to mind. That is because traditionally in classrooms all over the world students sat quietly at desks that were placed in rows as the teachers talked and talked. For the moments when students worked in groups, teachers placed them by ability level. Thankfully, less-traditional methods are sweeping through schools all over the world.

Methods are generally defined as the instructional decisions, approaches, procedures, or routines that expert teachers integrate into students' current abilities that aim to accelerate and enhance learning experiences. Here are some examples:

- Designing cooperative learning activities

- Optimizing access to technology

- Providing alternatives to visual information

- Providing alternatives to audio information

- Incorporating movement (get students up and out of their seats!)

- Providing opportunities for students to hear their own thoughts, self-regulate their learning, and then share their thinking out loud. Teachers must appreciate students' perspectives and provide opportunities for learners to value their own voice.

A UDL approach involves multiple means of presenting information to address the various ways students acquire knowledge and to keep the students engaged. For example, the lesson could include a short video clip and other visual representations of the concept. In addition, the class could view information from websites on a large computer screen, and books on the topic (that are appropriate for students at different reading levels) can be offered as resource materials (Sabia, 2008).

Educators who plan their lessons through a UDL lens stay flexible and open to meeting the specific needs of learners in their class. Flexible grouping is applied to help meet a variety of learning outcomes. For example, if the goal is to increase decoding and reading fluency, students can be placed in groups with peers who need to gain similar skills. If the learning target is to increase social interactions, mixed-ability levels can be grouped together to allow peers to learn from one another. In addition, a mixed ability grouping can provide opportunities for each member to express her personal strength. A student who is weak in decoding may be given the role as group illustrator as he listens to his peers share content knowledge. Educators must take a collaborative approach to developing methods in UDL style. The school's librarian or technology experts, as well as other teachers, are great resources in planning to meet the needs of variable learners.

## Assessments

An impulse response to the term *assessment* brings to mind the traditional paper and pencil, Scantron sheets, multiple choice, open-ended short response, and any end-of-a-unit or -chapter source for gaining information about what the learner has grasped. Many problems occur when we use only these summative kinds of assessments to determine whether students have learned. For starters, the content on the test will most likely not align exactly with the instructional process. Additionally, the formatting of the test and the mode of response will not align with the needs of all learners.

A UDL approach to assessment favors formative assessments that provide meaningful data on how students are performing—in real time—within the moments of the learning process. Formative assessments provide meaningful, process-oriented feedback to guide all learners to deeply understand themselves as learners. We can collect work samples such as exit tickets, graphic organizers, and writing samples to determine and provide evidence of students' abilities and applications. In addition, techniques are available to us that we can insert in the moments of instruction to gain instantaneous feedback on student engagement and performance. These techniques include ways of getting all students to respond—such as "thumbs up if you agree, thumbs down if you disagree."

Of course, the UDL approach also encourages using multiple means of ensuring that assessments are an accurate and fair measure of what students really know. A quick verbal check for understanding might be more effective than a written quiz, or vice versa. Assessments are also an integral part of sustaining perseverance and resiliency so learner in the room takes ownership of their learning as they push through the inevitable challenges that any successful learning experience endures.

# PRINCIPLES AND GUIDELINES: TOOLS FOR REFLECTION

Approaching curriculum with a flexible, open mind is a critical component to providing meaningful access to the content for all learners. The cycle of aligning high expectations for all students—through the flow of a proactively planned process with the four components of curriculum—has great promise for guiding variable learners to become expert learners who take charge of their learning and understand the process and strategies they need in any learning situation.

UDL can be such a natural part of any effective instructional process. Planning with UDL becomes second nature as teachers become mindful of how their natural routine and lesson planning process connect with honoring options for students to take in information, to apply strategies, and to express their understandings. Effective instruction allows for an active learning process that incorporates varying learning modalities to provide options for students to connect to learning in personal and meaningful ways. Planning lessons through the UDL lens can give teachers opportunities for creativity and flexibility in how they teach the curriculum. The lesson planning process evolves to provide consistent opportunities for teachers to choose how the learning process will unfold.

Let's pause here and reflect on one of your recent lessons—how did you and your co-teacher embed UDL into the process?

1. Consider multiple means of engagement:

   How did you optimize choice, vary demands and resources, optimize challenge, foster collaboration, or facilitate opportunities for students to self-reflect?

   _____

   _____

   _____

   _____

   _____

2. Consider multiple means of representation:

   How did you and your co-teacher vary the methods of presenting information, promote understanding of vocabulary, and activate background knowledge?

   _____

   _____

   _____

   _____

   _____

**3.** Consider multiple means of action and expression:

How did you and your co-teacher provide options for learners to respond, and implement multiple tools for listening, speaking, and writing? How did you guide goal-setting and strategic action steps toward goal achievement?

_____

_____

_____

_____

_____

You are getting the hang of it now—you're off to a great start! Let's consider a few examples of how the UDL Guidelines, in general, can be a powerful tool to light the way as teachers mindfully and meaningfully scaffold the learning process to support variable learners.

Now it's time for a more specific look at how UDL is explicitly embedded in any lesson plan. Let's look at this example of a seventh-grade English lesson that I implemented with one of my co-teachers. All of the students in this classroom were expected to read *Martin Eden* by Jack London. My co-teacher and I did not have official co-planning time, but we worked through email and through two brief before-school discussions to fine-tune our focus. This lesson demonstrates that any lesson may be illuminated with UDL as long as teachers provide opportunities for students to individually connect to the content through an active learning process. Take a look at the before and after UDL planning in Table 4.1.

**TABLE 4.1.** UDL—Before and After

| BEFORE UDL | AFTER UDL |
|---|---|
| **Goal** | **Goal** |
| Students will analyze and evaluate the literary text *Martin Eden* by Jack London and will respond to comprehension questions through written expression. | Students will analyze and evaluate the literary text *Martin Eden* by Jack London. Students will apply active reading strategies to guide their ability to interpret leveled comprehension questions as they locate text-based evidence and make inferences. Students will work independently or in pairs to express their understanding of the text. |

**TABLE 4.1.** UDL—Before and After *(continued)*

| BEFORE UDL | AFTER UDL |
|---|---|
| **Process** | **Process** |
| Students will sit at their desks arranged in rows. They are expected to follow along as the teacher reads the text aloud. The teacher will intermittently apply a think-aloud strategy to model how to annotate text while reading. Students are directed to reread the text on their own and add to their annotations to deepen their comprehension. | Prior to English class, I frontloaded the comprehension for a small group of students who had comprehension goals on their Individual Education Plans (IEPs). During this small-group study skills instruction, I modeled the purpose and the process of annotating text (See the Teacher Modeling Cue Card: How to Annotate a Text in this book's appendix) to deepen comprehension. I also modeled how readers mindfully monitor their comprehension by reading one section of the text and then generating questions, underlining, or jotting down key words in the margins. I gradually released responsibility to the students who became active readers throughout the process. Many students moved to using the Student Application Cue Card (also in this book's appendix) because they were becoming more independent. I also embedded decoding and vocabulary strategies to guide students to apply independently. Students engaged in peer collaborations through this scaffolded comprehension lesson. |
| | At the end of this lesson, students put their personalized annotated text in their English folder. |
| | When we met at the end of the day for English class, my small group of readers had their annotated text with them. The students' first reading with me worked to keep those who needed comprehension support engaged when the larger class met. Each student was an active part of the process that followed because they were not struggling with this complex text for the first time. They served as leaders during this whole-class lesson. |
| | The students' desks were arranged in groups of four or five to allow for cooperative learning activities. The lesson flowed with a balance of the teacher guiding the process of students' active reading. |

**TABLE 4.1.** UDL—Before and After *(continued)*

| BEFORE UDL | AFTER UDL |
|---|---|
| **Product** | **Product** |
| Students will demonstrate their comprehension by annotating and by answering multiple-choice questions. | Students demonstrated their comprehension by listening and speaking with teachers and peers through cooperative learning groups. All students needed to annotate the text through written expression, so scaffolds were put in place. These scaffolds included frontloading reading comprehension skills, teacher think-aloud, and opportunities for students to listen and speak within cooperative learning groups. In addition, they had the choice to sketch out their understanding of sections of the text. Students had the choice of working in pairs or going solo to respond to multiple-choice questions. |

This basic example illustrates a typical co-teaching situation where co-planning time was limited and the pacing of the content and skills teachers must teach moved at a rapid pace. Notice in this sample how any lesson can illuminate UDL when teachers remain mindful and dedicated to connect with each learner in the room with the UDL Guidelines leading the way. Table 4.2 shows more explicitly how this was accomplished.

**TABLE 4.2.** How UDL Was Naturally Embedded in the Table 4.1 Lesson

| MULTIPLE MEANS OF ENGAGEMENT: SUPPORT PURPOSEFUL, MOTIVATED LEARNERS |
|---|
| **Provide options for self-regulation.** |

- Promote expectations and beliefs that optimize motivation.
  - ▸ Goals were written with options for students to express their comprehension. For example, rather than requiring students to work independently to respond to multiple-choice questions, students were given options to express their comprehension through listening, speaking, drawing, and finally responding to those questions. This process kept students engaged and personally connected.

- Develop self-assessment and reflection.
  - ▸ Students were given the comprehension self-monitoring cue card to guide their thinking and the ability to share their voice during peer interactions and group discussions.

**TABLE 4.2.** How UDL Was Naturally Embedded in the Table 4.1 Lesson *(continued)*

| |
|---|
| **MULTIPLE MEANS OF ENGAGEMENT: SUPPORT PURPOSEFUL, MOTIVATED LEARNERS** |

**Provide options for sustaining effort and persistence.**

- Heighten salience of goals and objectives.

  ▸ Goals and academic vocabulary were made visible to students. For example, the standard was written on the board as well as on students' individual text copies:

  *Key Ideas and Details: Cite several pieces of textual evidence to support analysis of what the text says explicitly as well as inferences drawn from the text. The words, inferences, and text evidence were a natural part of students' language as they collaborated with peers.*

- Foster collaboration and community.

  ▸ Students engaged in think-pair-share along with whole-class discussion using the Accountable Talk protocol.

- Increase mastery-oriented feedback.

  ▸ Teachers provided specific feedback to students as they walked around the room. This served as a model to guide students' discussion with one another, as well as their ability to progress independently.

**Provide options for recruiting interest.**

- Optimize individual choice and autonomy.

  ▸ As part of the process, students were given choices of how to express their comprehension. Although all students needed to read the text and respond to multiple-choice questions, scaffolds were naturally embedded for anyone who chose to apply additional listening, speaking, or drawing opportunities to deepen their comprehension.

- Optimize relevance, value, and authenticity.

  ▸ Students had the opportunity to process the text and connect to what they were thinking through peer interactions, teacher modeling, and individual processing time.

- Minimize threats and distractions.

  ▸ A culture of learning has been established where students value their own thinking as well as the thinking of their peers. Meaningful class discussions unfolded.

| MULTIPLE MEANS OF ENGAGEMENT: SUPPORT PURPOSEFUL, MOTIVATED LEARNERS |
|---|

**Provide options for comprehension.**

- Guide information processing, visualization, and manipulation.

  ▸ The text was read in sections using the chunking strategy.

  ▸ Active reading strategies such as visualizing, making predictions, and making inferences were modeled and applied by students through peer collaborations, whole-class discussions, and individual student applications.

- Maximize transfer and generalization.

  ▸ Students applied their background knowledge of active reading strategies to reading this text. The skill of making inferences was discussed along with how monitoring our comprehension is helpful every time we read.

- Provide options for language, mathematical expressions, and symbols.

  ▸ Vocabulary was discussed in the context of reading and class discussions. Students were given the option to use their dictionary apps on an iPad to support their use of context clues within the text to define unknown words.

- Support decoding of text, mathematical notation, and symbols.

  ▸ Decoding strategies were modeled within the small-group instruction prior to the whole-class lesson. Students applied these strategies as needed within the whole-group setting.

**Provide options for perception.**

- Offer ways of customizing the display of information.

  ▸ The text was reformatted to incorporate wider margins and space between paragraphs to encourage students to read text in chunks, as well as monitor their progress after reading each section.

- Offer alternatives for auditory information.

  ▸ Teachers provided reformatted text and the visual self-monitoring comprehension cue card.

- Offer alternatives for visual information.

  ▸ Cooperative learning groups were formed for speaking and listening.

  ▸ The Accountable Talk technique was used to facilitate active listening and sharing of all student voices.

  ▸ Teacher think-alouds were used.

| MULTIPLE MEANS OF ACTION AND EXPRESSION: SUPPORTING STRATEGIC, GOAL-DIRECTED LEARNERS |
| --- |
| **Provide options for executive functions.** |
| • Guide appropriate goal-setting. |
|   ▸ The reading standard is easily embraced as learners personally connected within the natural learning environment. |
| • Support planning and strategy development. |
|   ▸ Active reading strategies were modeled, scaffolded, and applied. |
| • Enhance capacity for monitoring progress. |
|   ▸ Self-monitoring visual cue cards were offered. |
| **Provide options for expression and communication.** |
| • Use multiple tools for construction and composition. |
|   ▸ Listening, speaking, drawing, and multiple-choice questions were used. |
| • Build fluencies with graduated levels of support for practice and performance. |
|   ▸ Small-group instruction was used to review active reading strategies. |
|   ▸ Peer collaborations and individual student work opportunities were offered. |
| **Provide options for physical action.** |
| • Vary the methods for response and navigation. |
|   ▸ Oral expression, listening comprehension, sketching responses, and peer collaborations were among the methods tried. |
|   ▸ Dictionary apps on an iPad were offered. |

This lesson illuminates the beginning of a UDL journey for any teacher first starting out by connecting what he is already doing in the classroom to the principles of UDL. This example takes an average lesson where the goal of reading one text (in this case, *Martin Eden*) and completing multiple-choice questions were not an option for the teachers.

In this case, teachers must determine what options within the process they are able to scaffold in order for all students to achieve. By incorporating peer collaborations, a self-monitoring checklist, frontloading comprehension scaffolds for knocking down identified barriers, and expression options throughout the process of comprehension, the teachers ensured that all students were able to read the text and complete the multiple-choice questions that followed.

## THE CO-PLANNING PROCESS—UDL STYLE

Planning for the co-teaching process is typically one of the challenges that can easily be overcome when both teachers agree to do whatever it takes to make it work. Ideally, when both teachers are on board with their co-teaching assignment, the pathway is clear for a positive collaborative relationship. Yet the ideal is not necessary for success to be experienced. As long as one of the teachers is on board with co-teaching, the results may still be positive. So make a vow to be that teacher! Effective co-teachers are flexible. They focus on what's right for students and bounce back from any setbacks or frustrations that are a part of any co-teaching process.

▶ **Five Keys to Elevating Co-Teaching**

- Create a relationship based on mutual acceptance of each other's styles and expertise.

- Be flexible! Vary the implementation of co-teaching models to allow both teachers to remain active educators during all phases of the learning process.

- Maintain ongoing communications through face-to-face and digital opportunities to ensure both teachers share teaching responsibilities.

- Establish consistent planning routines, listen to each other's ideas, and combine the expertise of both co-teachers.

- Be open-minded enough to step out of personal comfort zones. Allow yourself to learn alongside your co-teaching partner. Look at instructional decisions in new ways.

Co-planning time tends to be quite a source of stress for so many. Far too often teachers do not have co-planning time set into their schedules. They do their best to make it work by meeting before school, after school, during lunch, or any time they can find. The secret to co-planning success isn't about being given a common planning time. It is about finding a way—and once this way is found—keeping it consistent.

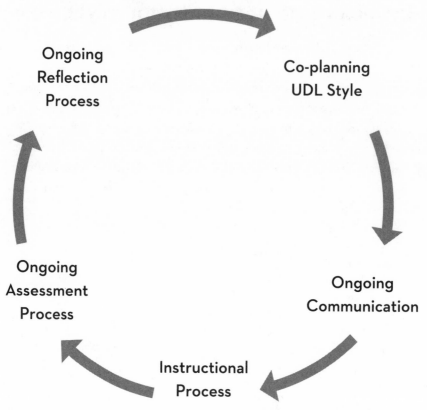

**FIGURE 4.2.** The phases of ongoing instructional improvement

The essence of co-teaching success consists of creating clear pathways for ongoing communication, collaborations, and compassion. When any co-teaching pair mindfully makes these three ideals their everyday focus for teaching and learning together, they will create a positive learning environment for all learners in the room—including the two teachers. When co-teachers are open-minded and open-hearted, they create a smooth pathway for co-teaching success. Embracing UDL can ensure there are multiple ways for creating this success. UDL provides a powerful framework to help co-teachers work together in ways that exhibit common goals and parity, as well as shared resources, responsibilities, and accountability for the achievements of all students in the room.

The key is flexibility both in perspective and planning:

**Flexible perspective:** Effective co-teachers have a clear but flexible idea of the many ways children learn. They extend their view by valuing the perspective of their co-teacher. They spend their time fine-tuning their strategy base for reaching all learners and doing the best they can to share their ideas with their co-teacher. They combine their ideas with the perspective of their co-teacher, and they plan all lessons around what they know about their students' interests and abilities.

**Flexible planning style:** Effective co-teachers use the principles of UDL to find multiple means of co-planning. They identify a means of communication that works for them. One year I was expected to co-plan with five different teachers on various subject areas. It was physically impossible to align schedules and personalities. I did the best I could in spite of the situation. With one co-teacher, we simply exchanged sticky notes with our planning ideas. With another teacher I used Google Docs to share our lesson planning ideas. With another teacher, I met a few mornings before class began. With another teacher, the best solution I found was to stop into the classroom and seize the moments to share a quick exchange—this quick check-in kept communication open and ongoing to the some degree—with my mind-set to always move forward.

As collaboration unfolds, each co-teacher's contributions are valued. For example, for one lesson, one teacher may contribute strong content knowledge and recognition networking, whereas the other teacher supports the content by contributing strong strategic networking—such as guided note-taking strategies or scaffolding vocabulary development by frontloading the vocabulary needed to comprehend the lesson. As co-teachers embrace the context of each lesson, they will naturally embrace the flexibility to share their expertise through multiple means of co-teaching. The general process of lesson planning becomes a proactive and personal consideration as the two teachers not only take their own styles and strengths into consideration, but also prepare for the variable learning strengths and needs along with additional scaffolds that meet the needs of the learners in their classroom. In short, a natural foundation for UDL can be created when co-teachers:

- Respect that each learner is an individual (including each teacher!).

- Embrace the talents, personalities, and expertise of both teachers.

- Foster active learning to make sure all learners have the opportunity to connect with the curriculum.

- Incorporate formative assessment as an ongoing barometer of students' performance.

# TAKEAWAY IDEAS

- Co-teaching can be elevated through the application UDL strategies. The UDL Guidelines are a meaningful tool to guide teachers as they embrace and naturally apply a UDL mind-set.

- Teachers may prepare students for UDL by setting the tone for an environment where all learners are free to take risks, ask questions, seek solutions, and collaborate. Teachers foster an environment where a growth mind-set is naturally embedded through shared positive belief systems.

- The four components of a UDL curriculum are goals, materials, methods, and assessment. As teachers think about meeting the needs of variable learners, they can use the UDL Guidelines to proactively (as well as flexibly) plan for multiple means of engagement, representation, action, and expression for each of the four components. Any lesson plan will naturally have evidence of UDL—however, in time, teachers become more mindful to plan ahead through a shared vision.

- Co-teaching and UDL share a natural connection through true collaborations. The UDL Guidelines serve as a visual reminder of the multiple ways co-teachers may express their individual expertise. Teachers use the UDL Guidelines to illuminate the multiple ways they may support the variable learners in their room.

- Co-teachers work together to break down co-teaching barriers, as well as any barriers that may be present within the instructional process. Co-teachers must maintain a solution-seeking mind-set as they plan for ways to meet the needs of variable learners in any classroom.

# STUDY GROUP QUESTIONS

1.  The curriculum is a living, breathing experience between teachers and students. Explain what this means to you. Provide at least one specific example from your classroom experiences.

2.  Think about a lesson that you will implement in the near future. What materials do you plan to use to deepen your students' personal connections to

learning? Explain why you selected certain materials. Be specific to the students in your room.

3.  What methods do you plan to incorporate that will support each student's connection to learning in your classroom?

4.  Provide one example of a summative assessment and one example of a formative assessment that you implement in your classroom. What purpose does each serve to inform your instruction? How do you and your co-teacher work together to maximize assessment as a means to inform your instruction and to help students to personally connect to their learning experiences?

5.  What types of barriers may show up in any co-teaching partnership? How can these barriers be knocked down?

6.  What types of barriers may be evident within the instructional moments for variable learners? How can teachers proactively plan and/or scaffold so these barriers do not exist?

# 5

# UDL in Action

AS YOU'VE SEEN IN EARLIER CHAPTERS, THE INSTRUCTIONAL CYCLE IN A UDL CLASSROOM DEPLOYS THE FOUR COMPONENTS OF CURRICULUM IN WAYS THAT ENHANCE LEARNERS' ABILITIES TO BUILD KNOWLEDGE (RECOGNITION NETWORKS), STRATEGIES AND SKILLS (STRATEGIC NETWORKS), AND THE MOTIVATION AND STAMINA TO LEARN (AFFECTIVE NETWORKS). As co-teachers put their lessons into action with the UDL principles in mind, they can create a masterful flow of meaningful learning opportunities for each student. In doing so, they show that they:

- Respect that each learner is an individual (including each teacher!)

- Embrace the talents, personalities, and expertise of both teachers

- Foster active learning to make sure all learners have the opportunity to connect with the curriculum

- Incorporate formative assessment as a barometer of students' performance

Let's look at an example of some scaffolding work I applied over the years. I created the following example to show how these experiences could look if applied during any one lesson with any co-teaching pairing. Be sure to notice how my co-teacher and I optimized our co-teaching moments in this example to provide UDL scaffolds that worked for all variable learners, while being flexible in the moments to provide scaffolds for a few students who required additional support through specially designed instructional supports. This example also depicts that being flexible in the moments and maintaining a UDL mind-set can transform any lesson plan (even if the co-teachers do not have co-planning time) into an accessible *and* meaningful learning experience.

# SCAFFOLDING FOR VARIABLE LEARNERS

Enter this sixth-grade science class...

As part of a unit on atmosphere and climate, the class was learning about cloud formation and types of clouds. My general education co-teaching partner Ms. Fields and I did not have any co-planning time, but she shared the content and the Microsoft PowerPoint visuals with me through email. As Ms. Fields entered the room, she and I welcomed the class, and then she launched the lesson through a class discussion supported by visual slides and a video presented on the SMART Board. I prepared a sheet of chart paper at the side of the room and was ready to model taking notes with a Cornell Note-Taking Outline (Figure 5.1).

**Cornell Notes Sheet**

Name:_____     Date: _____

Topic: _____     Text: _____

| Key Words, Phrases, or Questions | Notes |
|---|---|
| | |
| | |
| | |
| | |
| | |
| | |

Summary: Write 5–8 sentences to sum up your learning from these notes.

**FIGURE 5.1.** Cornell Note-Taking Outline

The instructional routine was already established at the beginning of the school year, so students were ready to decide how they planned to take notes. Some chose their notebooks (blank sheets of paper), and others chose the graphic organizer provided by the teachers. As Ms. Fields engaged the students through visual slides and videos, I added to her thinking by extending an idea and by paraphrasing key ideas for clarification and deeper comprehension.

Throughout the lesson, I modeled a note-taking technique for additional visual supports and organization. Following a 20-minute visual and auditory introduction to the types of clouds, Ms. Fields surprised everyone (including me!) and directed the students to use their class notes to write a paragraph answering the following questions:

1. What are clouds and how do they form?

2. Describe the four kinds of clouds. I jumped into solution-seeking mode because I immediately thought about the three students in the class who struggled significantly with writing.

As the students reviewed their notes, I quietly suggested to Ms. Fields that we provide a few minutes for students to collaborate prior to their actual writing time. She was hesitant because she wanted this to be an independent assessment, but she trusted my instincts—and she knew that the actual writing time would still be the students' independent work. I then instructed the students to move their desks into groups of four. I informed them that they had five minutes to discuss their thinking with one another before writing their individual paragraphs.

While students collaborated, I went over to Jason. He struggled with written expression but had a strong background knowledge base. In addition, I knew that Jason played the guitar and enjoyed creating songs. With a sticky note and pencil in hand, I sat with Jason and his group. After reading the comprehension questions, I asked the group: "What would a song about describing clouds sound like?" All of the students sat up a bit taller—all smiling. One said, "I have no idea!" Another student just began to sing the questions out loud. And then Jason chimed in, "Oh, that's easy..." And he began to whisper his song.

As he began to sing a few lyrics of his newly created "cloud song," the other kids in the group began to tap on their desks to provide some rhythm and cheer him on. Through this quiet excitement, I wrote some of the key words from Jason's song on a sticky note. After the two-minute song, the entire class clapped in honor of Jason's creativity. I then put the sticky note on Jason's desk and began to walk to another group. Jason and I exchanged a smile as Jason took the note and began to put his key words into his best paragraph writing. He was engaged!

Following this cooperative group discussion time, Eric, another student who struggled with writing, was able to compose a paragraph with his best efforts because the time with peers served to engage and empower his abilities. I needed to touch base with one more student in the class. Michael needed further support. He sat quietly and proudly as the rest of the class finished their writing.

He said he was done. Figure 5.2 shows his finished, independently written paragraph.

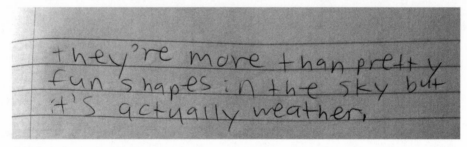

**FIGURE 5.2.** Michael's first effort

I acknowledged his efforts for executing this great beginning—but I let him know that I knew he had more to say. I guided him—on the spot—to add more details to his thinking by using the Question–Answer–Details (QAD) strategy. I did not have time to get fancy, so I took out a sheet of loose-leaf paper and provided him with a three-column visual to scaffold his thinking. He remembered learning this strategy with me earlier in the year in our study skills class period.

Once I quickly wrote the template, Michael immediately got to work. He first wrote the question, *What are clouds?* He wrote his answer—as seen on his first attempt in paragraph writing, Figure 5.2. *They're more than fun shapes in the sky.* And then he looked at me. I responded to his nonverbal inquiry by asking him, "What do you have to do next?" He responded, "Add details." I smiled and stayed quiet. He looked at his notes and then added, *They're made of tiny water droplets or ice crystals.* I said, "Now go back to your question—do you think your answer and detail answer the question?" He said, "Yes." I said, "Then keep going!" I gave him a thumbs up and walked away. He continued to use the QAD strategy to guide his thinking to go deeper (Figure 5.3).

Class time ended and Michael did not yet finish his paragraph. But he was engaged! This strategy guided him to organize his thoughts on paper as a scaffold to writing the paragraph on a blank sheet of paper. He asked for a pass to come back at lunch to finish writing his paragraph. His final paragraph (Figure 5.4) was completed in 15 minutes.

| Q | A | D |
|---|---|---|
| what are clouds | They're more than fun shapes in the sky. | They're made of tiny water droplets or ice crystals |

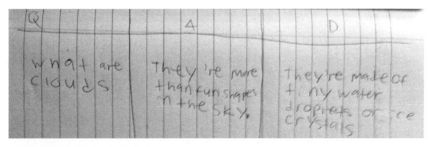

**FIGURE 5.3.** Michael adds detail.

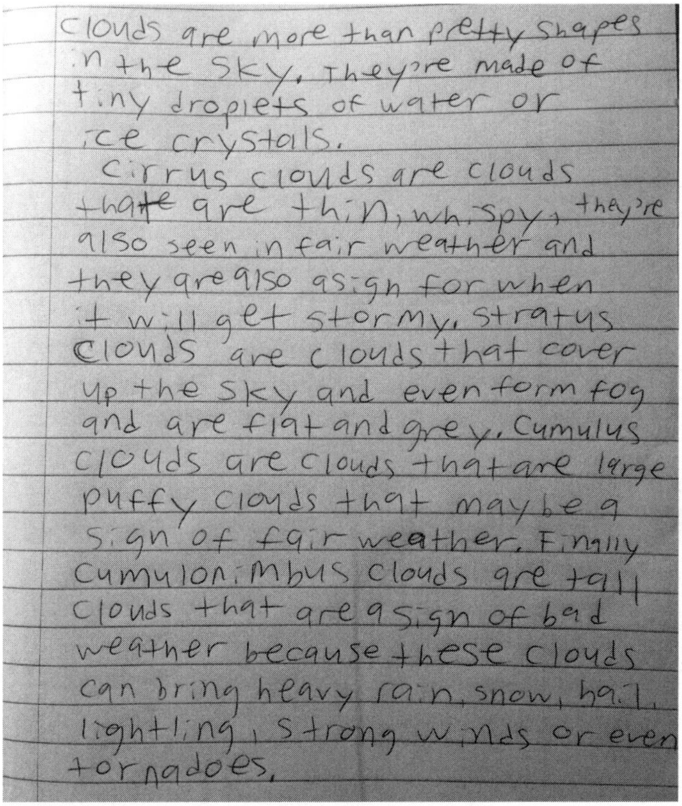

clouds are more than pretty shapes in the sky. They're made of tiny droplets of water or ice crystals.
Cirrus clouds are clouds that are thin, whispy, they're also seen in fair weather and they are also asign for when it will get stormy. Stratus clouds are clouds that cover up the sky and even form fog and are flat and grey. Cumulus clouds are clouds that are large puffy clouds that may be a sign of fair weather. Finally Cumulonimbus clouds are tall clouds that are a sign of bad weather because these clouds can bring heavy rain, snow, hail, lightling, strong winds or even tornadoes.

**FIGURE 5.4.** Michael's final paragraph

The power of co-teaching is highlighted in this example on so many levels. For starters, rather than spin our wheels about not having consistent co-planning time, we combined our efforts by remaining flexible in the moments. In this particular lesson, Ms. Fields presented the material in multiple ways through options of perception (visual and auditory). I added additional visual supports and strategic thinking by modeling a note-taking technique using a strategy that was previously taught to the class. In her last-minute decision to embed a formative assessment writing sample, Ms. Fields did not stop to think that three students in the class would need additional supports. But with the power of two teachers in the room, this was not a problem. Ms. Fields trusted in our various modes of expertise as well as in our co-teaching process.

Ms. Fields was flexible to go with my lead to continue guiding all learners, while including additional specialized supports to a few students. Not only does cooperative learning work very well to allow students to take charge of their own learning, but it also gives teachers time to support individuals and small groups as needed. This example demonstrates how co-teachers can forge a bond of collaboration and flexibility as they trust the instincts and expertise of one another—within the real-time instructional moments.

## ▶ Multiple Means of Co-Teaching Effectiveness
### Engagement

- Provide ongoing personal and collaborative opportunities to optimize the motivation to co-teach. When teachers focus on the goals of the students and of the curriculum, they maintain a clear focus.

- Include mastery-oriented feedback. Co-teachers should be transparent with one another. Share your thoughts to allow for open, honest collaborations.

- Provide opportunities for each teacher to share his choice of instructional methodologies and routines. Value the opinion and perspective of one another.

- Create a co-teaching check-in process to assess your own co-teaching practices.

- Use Strengths-based Check-in Reflection (see this book's appendix) for a quick reflective process that can increase communication and coping skills to keep the co-teaching relationship moving in positive directions.

## Representation

- Make sure you both have a clear understanding of the varied co-teaching models.

- Communicate through discussions in person, or using email, Google Docs, sticky notes, and so forth to maximize ideas for promoting instructional content and processes.

## Action and Expression

- Set goals for your co-planning and for your instructional processes. Goal-setting on a weekly basis will keep the goals reasonable and meaningful.

- Share strategies to support various pathways of learning along with supporting the expertise of each co-teacher.

- Use a check-in process to monitor the effectiveness of your instructional planning and implementations.

It is important for co-teachers to remember that the instructional decisions they make create strong experiences and students' belief systems in themselves as learners. Students like Michael and Jason define themselves as learners through a process of strategic, purposeful actions rather than by the finished product alone. Through the flexibility and goal-oriented nature of UDL, learners are empowered. In addition, co-teachers have the opportunity to create learning experiences through the privilege of a co-teaching environment.

Effective co-teaching experience begins with teachers who share a vision for the purpose and goals of learning while combining their individual expertise. It leads to a meaningful process that supports active learners who all strive to reach specific learning goals through a process that makes sense for them. Finally, throughout the entire learning process, both teachers are monitoring (and guiding students to self-monitor) their performance. It is through these keen observations and monitoring that learning becomes intentional and motivational. These observations and evidence of students' performance guides all instructional decisions in real time.

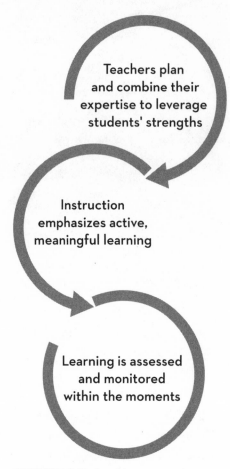

**FIGURE 5.5.** Co-teaching process

When co-teachers plan and combine their expertise, they are following their general lesson plan outline. They consider the goals for the lesson and the instructional decisions about what strategies they will use to keep the process of the lesson moving. In addition to the process of instruction, they consider the way(s) they will incorporate formative assessment to monitor the students' abilities and performance. When each teacher adds her ideas for how to meet the needs of each learner, the chance for student achievement is greater. When movement of decisions and responsibilities between co-teachers exists, we can identify ways where co-teachers provide multiple means of co-teaching effectiveness to optimize co-teaching through a UDL lens.

## ▶ Using Formative Assessments

It is so important to include formative assessment as a natural part of your instructional process. Summative assessments alone, such as end-of-chapter or unit tests, do not demonstrate students' abilities and true levels of understanding. Just think about Jason from our example earlier. If we used the written paragraph alone as a summative assessment, Jason would have appeared to not know the content, therefore becoming trapped in a misunderstood ability cycle. But because we made time to include a scaffolding formative assessment process, we included the opportunity for him to express his knowledge of the content in a way that worked for him—which led him to be able to demonstrate, in writing, that he knew the content. His weakness in writing was no longer a barrier to his ability to demonstrate his knowledge of the content.

Establishing a consistent formative assessment cycle does wonders to demystify the process of aligning our instructional decisions with the specific needs of variable learners. The ultimate goal of formative assessment is to guide students to achieve. To make this personal achievement happen, teachers must be mindful of student performance along the way. Teachers use what they learn about student performance to inform their instruction.

In the case of Michael, I knew based on Michael's prior performance that he needed additional supports to bridge the gap between his knowledge of cloud formation and his ability to add details and express himself in writing. And so with the UDL mind-set, we made the time for additional scaffolds (specifically in Michael's case, the QAD strategy). The evidence of his finished paragraph demonstrated the progress he made in his abilities to add more details and express his ideas in writing. Without looking at Michael's previous performance, my co-teacher and I would just be spinning our wheels throwing writing tasks his way without knowing how to meet his needs. Michael's performance informed our instructional decisions.

There are many ways to embed a meaningful formative assessment cycle. The following strategy keeps the four components of a UDL curriculum at the forefront to ensure mindful flexibility. It has worked for me time and time again—in all variations of my co-teaching experiences.

1. Set the goal. What learning goal are you assessing the achievement of?

2. What materials and methods will be needed to guide student learning?

3. Describe how student performance will be evaluated (for example, rubrics, work samples, observation checklists, anecdotal notes). A combination of sources is preferred to provide consistency in your understanding of students' abilities.

4. Collect data and student work samples.

5. Analyze the patterns of student performance. Are many students struggling in the same areas? If so, what does that tell you about your instructional decisions? If not, what does that tell you about individual learners?

6. Reflect. Ask yourself if your formative assessment choices are a good way of assessing students' knowledge and skills. Make sure you are including students in the process, so they may learn to self-monitor their learning within a strong formative assessment cycle.

7. Plan for the next steps.

## ELEVATING CO-TEACHING INSTRUCTION WITH UDL REFLECTIONS

The UDL journey is a unique experience for everyone. A teacher knows that a UDL mind-set is achieved when UDL feels naturally embedded in the instructional planning, implementation, and assessment cycles. It is never something separate or added on to a lesson. It will feel like a natural cycle of meaningful learning where all learners in the room are active participants as thinkers, speakers, and listeners who flow through multiple means of learning opportunities that optimize personal achievements.

At first it will likely feel like more work since you are required to become more mindful of your applications. The implementation of the UDL Guidelines may feel like a checklist to accomplish, but with practice, it becomes a natural flow of learning as it weaves naturally through your instructional decisions and applications. Students and teachers respond positively to this stimulating learning environment because all thinking is valued—all students feel the presence of opportunities to personally connect to the curriculum. UDL naturally flows within meaningful learning experiences that truly strengthen each student's relationship with themselves as learners.

## ▶ How Administrators Can Support Positive Co-teaching Instructional Practices

- Provide ongoing professional development through online and face-to-face opportunities.

- Build in time for creating communities of practice where co-teachers may collaborate. Creating this space for co-teachers to knock down any co-teaching barriers can make instructional time relevant and meaningful. In addition, teachers should make time to proactively plan and also reflect on the lessons. Use the Busting Co-teaching Barriers template in the appendix to spark this planning and reflective time.

- Provide specific feedback following ongoing walk-throughs of the classrooms. Notice the following:

  - Did both teachers take an active role in the learning process?

  - Did the students connect with both teachers?

  - Did the teachers complement each other in ways that sparked the learning for everyone?

  - Were a variety of students' needs met through the expertise of both teachers?

  - Did the teachers implement one or more co-teaching models within the time of your walk-through?

  - What went well? What would you suggest the teachers could work on?

Once this UDL lens is established, co-teachers begin to communicate in ways that value *how* students are grappling with the content, not just keeping a focus on the outcome as an endpoint, but rather as a process of ongoing learning and achieving. Co-teachers should discuss and co-plan the ways to design lessons so that the content is *accessible* to all students as well as *rigorous* in that it creates personal connections and deeper learning. For example, Joey is an eighth-grade student who is reading on a sixth-grade reading level. Here's what a quick co-teaching debrief during a low-tech UDL lesson could look like:

Teacher 1: "I think that lesson on Reconstruction went well—all students had the opportunity to access the reading we needed them to accomplish."

Teacher 2: "Yes, I agree! Joey was able to maintain his focus because we created the option for the students to view the video at station #1— that really provided the background knowledge they all needed. And it helped Joey to connect what we were learning with what he already knows about the Civil War."

Teacher 1: "And when it came time for the reading, I am so glad we didn't have the students just read silently at their seats. Setting up the options for some to read silently, others to read in small groups, and yet others to join one of us in a more guided reading experience really made the difference!"

Teacher 2: "Yes, I'm glad Joey chose to read with his peers in the small group. He really followed along, and he was the perfect note-taker for the group."

With a UDL lens, the focus is on teachers reflecting on their instructional decisions to create clear access between each learner in the room and the content itself. In the previous example, Joey's reading level was a barrier to his accessing the material on his own. Yet through proactive planning, the co-teachers worked together to create a process that allowed for the material to reach learners in a variety of ways.

In the beginning of this book, we looked at two classrooms where teachers implemented the same lesson in very different ways. What was your first impression? Did both classrooms apply effective instruction? Be specific; explain why you think the way you do. Are you able to identify the co-teaching models of instruction that each co-teaching pair applies? Are you able to identify the UDL components? You've had some time to think about it. Feel free to look through this book to refresh as you begin to put specific language into describing what was happening in each classroom. Let's first refresh our memories of what happened in these two classrooms.

## Revisiting the Two Classrooms from Chapter 1

Enter co-taught classroom #1. Any grade—any subject—anywhere. Focus Anchor Standard: Determine central ideas or themes of a text and analyze their development; summarize the key supporting details and ideas.

The class of 25 students is sitting in rows listening to one of the teachers reading aloud from a chapter book. The teacher walks up and down the rows as she dramatically reads and makes eye contact with each student. She uses her voice to guide students to visualize character traits and story elements. She pauses every so often to remind students to close their eyes and visualize. There are no external visuals. There are no additional materials. Just one teacher, rows of desks, and students sitting at their desks encouraged using their imaginations. The students are visibly attentive as they watch the teacher read with some dramatic displays of expression and voice. A few chuckles can be heard around the room as she reads.

The second co-teacher is at the back of the room; she is following along in her copy of the book, ready to take over the reading as the first teacher nods and smiles her way. Before this second teacher reads, she asks the students a few guided questions to make sure they are following along and understanding what's happening in the text so far. These questions are orally presented to the entire class. There are no visuals and no additional materials. The students are still sitting in their seats. This teacher also walks around the room, so all of the students are once again seemingly attentive. A few students eagerly raise their hands. A few students quickly look down at their shoes as the teacher walks passed their desk. One or two students are called on, the answers to the comprehension questions are revealed, and the teacher succinctly sums up what has happened in the reading so far. She is ready to continue reading. Students once again follow the teacher's movements and smile as she, too, reads with dramatic expression. At the end of the reading, the first teacher says, "Great class today! Be ready for a quiz on this chapter at the beginning of our next class." The teacher quickly directs the class to transition to the next subject.

Now let's enter co-taught classroom #2 to see the same lesson. The class of 25 students is sitting in groups of five. Students' desks are facing one another. The first teacher is up at the SMART Board reviewing some active reading strategies. She opens a discussion on how to annotate the text to deepen the readers' comprehension. The second co-teacher takes the lead and tells the class they will be practicing this annotation skill during the reading of a short paragraph, as she models her thinking and annotating. The first co-teacher asks each group to discuss what they noticed about the teacher's think-aloud and how it connected to their own thinking. Students were given a few minutes to discuss. Following a quick debriefing, one co-teacher introduced the text they were about to read. She offered students a choice. They could read the text, while following along with text-to-speech software, they could engage in a shared reading with one of the teachers reading aloud, they could use iPads to read the text electronically with the use dictionary apps, they could partner-read with a peer, or they could go solo and read silently. This may sound like a lot of choices, but these students are used to making decisions about how they will learn best. Their opinions, feelings, moods, and voice are valued each day.

The classroom is set up for the ease of arranging desks and the flexibility for students to choose the process for engaging in the learning experience. After moving easily around the room, the students were ready to begin the reading task within a few minutes. The teachers did not need to assign student groups. Thirteen students chose to go solo and complete the reading assignment successfully on their own—while using the iPads occasionally to support their vocabulary knowledge. Five students sat in a group with one of the co-teachers reading as they followed along. Two students chose to partner-read, whereas five students chose to go to the computer lab where the librarian set them up to read along using Google text-to-speech supports. The other co-teacher was monitoring the engagement of all students and implementing supports, as needed. She noticed that all students were engaged and taking charge of their own learning.

## Let's Discuss!

Now, look back at what you wrote down after your initial thinking in Chapter 1. Are you able to add to your thoughts now? How has your thinking about UDL and co-teaching changed after what you've read so far?

Complete these sentences:

I used to think UDL was _____.

Now I think _____.

I used to think co-teaching was _____.

Now I think _____.

UDL can elevate instruction in inclusive classrooms with co-teachers when

_____.

Now that you have a deeper sense of your co-teaching with the UDL framework, let's take a look at the two classrooms we just entered.

Keep in mind that what I'm sharing here are just my ideas—there are no right or wrong responses in our UDL reflections. It's just important to get the conversations started and the collaborations going. So, let's begin!

### Evidence of Effective Instruction in Both Classrooms

*First classroom:* Teachers use their voice and eye contact to connect and engage learners. One of the teachers stopped to summarize key points and allowed learners time to process what was happening so far in the text.

*Second classroom:* Students are in groups rather than in rows. This seating arrangement encourages peer interactions and collaboration. Cooperative learning activities were planned with the learners at the center of the instruction. They are given choices, time to process, time to move, time to collaborate, and time to engage in meaningful tasks that align with the learning goals. All learners are supported in ways that challenge them while supporting their thinking and learning to move them beyond the point where they started. Technology was used in effective ways to support learning opportunities.

### Evidence of Co-teaching Models

*First classroom:* One may argue this is team teaching because teachers are technically teaching together—they each have a role, and they are both active. Another may argue this is one-teach, one-assist because as one teacher leads the class, the other is somewhere in the room—hopefully monitoring students' performance in some way. And yet another may argue that there is no clearly defined co-teaching model at all. It could appear that these teachers are just taking turns. If they are just taking turns, then co-teachers, beware! Do not fall into the taking-turns trap. Ask yourself, *Is there any specialized instruction going on? Is there evidence that the special education teacher has embedded some strategies to support learning?* In classroom #1, there is some evidence that the second teacher included processing time to summarize and review key points. But is that enough? You be the judge.

*Second classroom:* This seems to be team teaching at its best! Both teachers introduce the lesson, model strategic thinking, and allow students time to collaborate and process in meaningful ways to allow each to personally connect. In addition, once students move into groups of their choice, they are all working toward the same high standards, but they are given the opportunity to engage in the learning process in ways that support and challenge them to learn the material. One co-teacher facilitates the learning in a small group, whereas the other teacher monitors the whole class and supports as needed. This could be viewed as the workshop model allowing students to apply strategies taught to them. This is clearly a positive learning environment for all.

## Evidence of UDL Components

First classroom:

> *Engagement:* Teachers use their voice and facial expressions. One teacher embeds time to process and monitor comprehension through summarizing key points.

> *Representation:* Content is presented primarily through auditory modality with some visual as the teachers display the reading in dramatic ways.

> *Action and Expression:* Whole-class discussion emphasizes oral expression. This may leave many students behind if auditory processing is not strong. In addition, all students will be given a quiz during the next class. But ask yourself, *was each learner supported to comprehend the text?*

Second classroom:

*Engagement:* Varied resources are used to optimize learning. Peer collaboration is fostered as well as students' abilities to reflect and connect with the learning process.

*Representation:* Learning is supported through guided scaffolds to increase comprehension and extend background knowledge. Alternatives to auditory and visual information were naturally embedded.

*Action and Expression:* Methods of actions and responses are varied through the use of multiple media. Students' strategic thinking was supported through a variety of tools and technologies. Students were given the opportunities to monitor their learning by allowing them to make choices and monitor their comprehension and performance throughout the learning experience.

# TAKEAWAY IDEAS

- Co-teachers must work together to create a solid foundation of respect for one another's areas of expertise. Together they can maximize opportunities to infuse the learning environment with UDL opportunities to support each learner in the room.

- Co-teachers must be flexible in the moments of teaching to allow for necessary changes in the way students perceive, process, and express the information.

- Co-teachers must be keen observers in order to notice the specific ways students are performing. Ideally, co-teachers should proactively co-plan. Yet it is evident that there will be times when flexible instructional decisions must be made during teaching.

- General education teachers must provide space for the special education teacher to weave in additional UDL scaffolds and specially designed instructional strategies to meet the needs of students in the moment.

- Both teachers should consider the learning goals and connect to students' abilities to create opportunities for students to personally connect to learning. Embracing multiple means of co-teaching effectiveness allows the talents and expertise of both teachers to shine as they engage in a co-planning and teaching cycle that includes UDL principles and maintaining high expectations for all learners.

# STUDY GUIDE QUESTIONS

1. Think of a recent lesson that demonstrates one way you and your co-teacher planned for individual learner opportunities to connect with the lesson goal, content, and materials. What UDL principle does it connect with? Specifically, how did you incorporate the UDL Guidelines to optimize learning for your students?

2. Think about how the learning process was made accessible and meaningful for Michael and Jason in the example described in this chapter. What UDL principles and guidelines connect with the success of this lesson? How do you connect your class and your students to this example?

3. Review the multiple means of co-teaching effectiveness. How can you incorporate one new way to increase your co-teaching with UDL experience?

4. Explain the value of providing opportunities for students to self-regulate their learning. How does this connect to specific students in your class? How do you encourage students to self-regulate?

5. How can effective formative assessments empower students and elevate co-teaching?

6. Describe one way you embed high expectations for all learners in your classroom. Be specific. What is one way you may incorporate the co-teaching models as you plan to amplify an upcoming lesson?

7. Explain how UDL, SDI, and co-teaching connect in ways to elevate instruction in inclusive settings.

8. How do you connect with the two classrooms we just reflected on?

9. Share one of your lessons from the past week—how have you and your co-teacher included co-teaching models, UDL, and SDI?

10. Think about an upcoming lesson—how can you naturally embed UDL into your co-teaching structure? How will you ensure that UDL and specialized instruction is included to support the needs of each learner?

# 6

# Empowering Students as UDL Partners

ONE OF THE MOST POWERFUL ASPECTS OF USING THE UDL GUIDELINES IS THE WAY THEY CONNECT US TO LEARNERS IN THE CLASSROOM. As we include specific strategies to guide strategic, goal-oriented learners, we automatically engage them by promoting high expectations and self-empowerment. In addition, as we weave in multiple ways of action and expression, we touch upon multiple ways of representing materials to meet the needs of the variability in our classrooms.

The strategies shared in this book may elevate the instructional process as two teachers join forces to make meaningful learning happen. Learners who are purposeful and resourceful know where to seek resources, and who they can go to with questions and comments to seek more information. They become motivated and knowledgeable by setting goals and applying strategies that guide their thinking and confidence to be the absolute best version of themselves as possible. You might begin the process of recruiting students as your UDL partners by sharing with them the Letter to Learners and Letter to Parents and Caregivers, both found in the appendix.

# PREPARING STUDENTS FOR THE UDL EXPERIENCE

Just as we prepare students to embrace two teachers in the room as a positive aspect to their learning process, we must also naturally embed their abilities to embrace a UDL mind-set. Let's start out here with one of my favorite quotes I like to share with students:

> We have work to do. You can't just sit in a seat and grow smart. . .
> I promise, you are going to do, and you are going to produce. And I am not going to let you fail.
>
>> —Marva Collins, teacher, leader, and activist (Collins & Tamarkin, 1982)

From the beginning of our learning days together, students know that learning is an active process—it is a personal, emotion-filled, learning process. And I, as their teacher, will do all I can to support, guide, and nudge them forward in positive ways to embrace themselves as learners. Failure is a positive aspect within a successful learning process, and students must embrace that their efforts and learning decisions are fueled by persistence and resiliency. I incorporate the words of Abdul Kalam to prepare students to allow positive learning energy to flow naturally throughout the school year:

> If you fail, never give up because F.A.I.L. means "First Attempt In Learning." End is not the end, in fact E.N.D. means "Effort Never Dies." If you get No as an answer, remember N.O. means "Next Opportunity." So let's be positive.
>
>> —Abdul Kalam, author, scientist, former president of India (Kalam & Tiwari, 1999)

Once the tone is set and this growth mind-set view is embraced, students are ready to see that learning is an active process incorporating the multiple means of engagement, representation, and action and expression. Table 6.1 depicts how I share my UDL view as I launch a class discussion to hear students' connections, questions, and ideas.

**TABLE 6.1.** Introducing Students to UDL

| MULTIPLE MEANS OF ENGAGEMENT | MULTIPLE MEANS OF REPRESENTATION | MULTIPLE MEANS OF ACTION AND EXPRESSION |
|---|---|---|
| Each of you will have opportunities to connect with what we learn.<br><br>You will be a part of setting personal and group learning goals that will guide our plan of action for learning.<br><br>You will participate in a variety of activities that will create opportunities for you not only to be inspired, but to also inspire others.<br><br>Each of you will have the opportunity to take charge of your own learning. | We will do our best to offer all material in a variety of ways. Sometimes visuals such as graphic organizers, maps, or videos will help you to learn something deeper.<br><br>You will also have the opportunity to tell us if you need to see a topic or idea in another way. | Each learner in the room has unique talents and abilities.<br><br>You will have many opportunities to collaborate with one another.<br><br>Other times, you will be given the opportunity to work solo—to guide you to make sense of the material.<br><br>Throughout the year you will have a variety of opportunities to express what you know about the topics we study. There will be opportunities to speak, write, create multimedia products, act delete, sketch, and tap into our natural abilities to communicate our love of learning. |

Reading picture books aloud is another effective way to relax and guide learners to connect to a specific concept you are teaching. In the case of UDL, two picture books by Peter Reynolds are a perfect way to introduce the idea of UDL to students in any grade.

- *The North Star* is a book that expresses the fact that every individual is on a journey (and learning path) and requires different opportunities and decisions along the way to achieve personal success.

- *Ish* shares a beautiful story of the value and necessity that struggling along one's learning path holds for true personal success to happen. It guides learners to value the creative side of action and expression, along with adopting a growth mind-set along the way.

These stories could launch meaningful class discussion in how UDL will be a natural part of the learning process in your classroom.

## SUPPORTING ENGAGEMENT

As co-teachers, we want to create a relaxed learning environment that eliminates threats and distractions. The learning place is a comfortable one where each learner can share her thinking and listen to the thinking of one another. Engaged learners feel a sense of independence as their level of confidence builds. They do not panic when they do not know something, but rather they are motivated by the challenge to seek answers. They know they are in a class that provides the structure and the strategies to guide their autonomy. They are active listeners because they do not feel the anxiety of being called on out of the blue. And if they are called on, they feel comfortable taking a risk and sharing out loud. They are relaxed enough to connect with the learning so they may gain the knowledge and strategic thinking needed to apply in all learning situations—not just for the moments of that class.

Picture this: You arrange your desks in pairs, in small groups of four, or in rows. You decide the arrangement of the desks depending on your lesson. You make certain to keep the movement of furniture easy and natural. You and your co-teacher (any co-teacher) are on the move as you work in tandem to engage students with the process of learning. There are conversations between the two of you as you model the thinking and actions needed in a given learning situation. You also make time for learners to have conversations with one another as they process, solve, and push through challenges to complete academic tasks.

Other times, students are quietly working at their seats as they individually apply strategies to deeply connect with the materials and content. You and your co-teacher share the responsibility of representing the content with a keen sense of promoting strategic learners through a mindful emphasis on the process. An objective observer may be able to tell that one teacher is taking charge of teaching the content, and the other teacher is zooming in to teach the steps for strategic thinking. Yet this observer may not know which is the general education teacher and which is the special education teacher because they are both flexible in shifting the roles and responsibilities depending on the context of the lesson. The classroom is noisy in a purposeful manner. You hear students thinking out loud. You hear teachers guiding students' thoughts through effective questioning that deepens their engagement along the learning process. You hear students saying comments like, "Is class over already! That went fast!" Students in this class are accustomed to daily opportunities to meaningfully process information and make informed decisions.

One year as I launched a UDL-friendly environment at the beginning of the year with my fifth-grade co-teacher, we gave students a quick writing warm-up exercise. Students were given a few minutes to select a topic, and then had five minutes to write about their selected topic. One student sat quietly at his desk without writing. When I went over to check with him, he told me, "I've just never been given the choice before. I am usually forced to just write about a topic that a teacher tells me to write about. It's not easy to think about a topic." Since I knew this student's interests, I was able to take the time to weave a few questions to guide his focus. He selected a topic and began to write.

The seeds of engagement were planted with those simple steps. A UDL classroom provides a rich learning environment where making decisions and sharing one's voice is within one's natural comfort zone of learning. The flow of a co-taught UDL classroom is smooth and relaxed. It includes ongoing planning and sharing, communication, learning process, assessment, and reflection. It is a process where each learner (including the teachers) have opportunities to think, share their voice, and value their thinking, as well as the perspective of others in the room.

One of the most important teaching responsibilities is the necessity to guide students to actively monitor and regulate their learning process. The idea of self-regulation refers to the degree to which students can regulate the process of their thinking, motivation, and learning behaviors (Pintrich & Zusho, 2002). The following are six phases of the learning process that learners need to monitor:

1. Setting goals

2. Identifying and applying strategies used to achieve those goals

3. Seeking and utilizing appropriate resources

4. Applying effort

5. Being receptive and responsive to external feedback

6. Creating the result and product from the learning

Teachers must be mindful to guide students to depend on their own instincts as they plan, implement, and monitor their learning. Co-teachers find additional value in this because students who have been accustomed to learning through their focus on a specific disability may easily adopt a "learned helplessness" attitude, which can lead them to fall into unproductive learning traps. These students must work harder to achieve learning goals. Unless the right strategies and supports are in place, these students may not gain the stamina to push through the additional challenges.

As co-teachers make self-regulation a strong learning focus, these students have the opportunity to develop positive learning behaviors as they work toward their personal best versions of becoming expert learners.

## SUPPORTING PERCEPTION THROUGH MULTIPLE MEANS OF REPRESENTATION

As co-teachers, we want to keep in mind the many ways information can be presented so that learners can access it and, most important, attach meaning to it in personal ways. For example, we can consider additional visuals and auditory, depending on the context of the lesson. We can consider the formatting of text to ensure that the appearance of the information is perceptible to each student. For example, is the font too small or too large? Is there enough space in the margins to allow for accessible tracking of the sentences? Co-teachers have the additional opportunity to combine their knowledge of multiple tools for supporting and increasing vocabulary and concept development.

## SUPPORTING ACTION AND EXPRESSION

Co-teachers can again combine their efforts to support successful goal-setting and strategy development. Typically, the general education teacher can combine his content-area learning goal with the special education teacher's knowledge of individual students' IEP goals and goals for strategic process development. The special education teacher can apply her expertise in progress monitoring to guide formative, "in the moments" process so that students are able to gain information, process it, and self-regulate for deeper understandings.

This is an important part of co-teaching the UDL way, because students' needs regarding executive functioning will vary significantly across any classroom—but especially the inclusive classroom. Executive functioning is a part of every person's daily thinking, learning, and acting, yet we usually take these skills for granted. Teachers in the upper grades usually expect students to be able to make decisions, plan their study habits, and prepare for homework and long-term assignments. In addition, they expect students to keep their notebooks neat and organized and come to class with all the materials they need. Yet these expectations should not be taken lightly. These are skills that more often than not students in inclusive settings need support to master. Think about the last time you needed to plan, organize, set goals, monitor your progress, or regulate your behavior in some way. That's right—the last time will inevitably be today! Each day, successful people accomplish tasks due to effective executive functioning skills. For example, these skills allow us to:

- Make decisions and plan ahead

- Manage our time

- Multitask and keep track of our progress

- Connect past experiences to new learning

- Evaluate ideas

- Reflect on our work to monitor our performance and to set goals based on that performance

- Seek out resources when we need help to accomplish something

- Apply pragmatic skills during discussions that tell us when it's our turn to speak and when we need to wait for our turn

In short, executive functioning skills allow us to organize our thinking and our actions to plan and implement tasks along a successful process toward completion.

# REVISITING UDL AND THE CO-TEACHING MODELS

To help you elevate co-teaching with UDL, I have identified a few key components in the planning and implementation process:

1.  Incorporate a variety of co-teaching models.

2.  Embed UDL scaffolds and strategies.

3.  Provide further explicit instruction and scaffolds through specially designed instruction (SDI) to address additional specific individual student needs according to Individual Education Plans (IEPs).

As we mentioned earlier in the book, the co-teaching models alone are not enough to provide meaningful instruction. The models simply organize a structure for us to be flexible with the way we group our learners for specific lessons as we design instruction to connect each student with the learning experience. In addition, the co-teaching models allow each teacher's expertise to rise to the forefront of instructional time.

At this point in the book, I believe readers have the idea that co-teachers have seen UDL as a way of creating a relaxed learning environment in which students not only access the curriculum and materials, but also engage in meaningful, rigorous learning activities. Learning is not a chore—it is an experience full of positive emotions as learners push through comfort zones and challenges because their teachers designed instruction with appropriate scaffolds and relevant content and materials. With this in mind, I would like to propose yet another teaching technique that could empower the co-teaching experience—UDL style. This teaching structure does not quite fit into any one co-teaching model we've discussed so far. The next section shows how to make our learners part of our co-teaching team through a *workshop structure*.

# MAKING LEARNERS PART OF THE CO-TEACHING TEAM: APPLYING A WORKSHOP STRUCTURE

We understand that effective teachers know what skills their students are able to perform independently (the *zone of actual development*, or *ZAD*). Knowing each student's entry point for learning (ZAD), effective teachers plan to guide their students beyond their ZAD and nudge them toward their *zone of proximal development* (*ZPD*; Vygotsky, 1978). In addition to the co-teaching models discussed so far, the workshop structure deserves careful consideration.

A workshop model embraces the powerful "I do, we do, you do" scaffolded structure developed by Vygotsky (1978; Fig. 6.1). Let's consider the following general lesson outline using a workshop structure (for any subject or grade level).

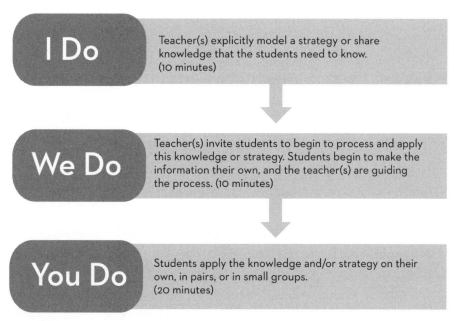

**FIGURE 6.1.** Lesson outline for scaffolding learners' independence

This workshop structure has boundless possibilities for co-teachers. The first "I Do!" section may be structured using one of the six co-teaching models discussed earlier. For example, co-teachers may decide to parallel teach the first 10 minutes, or they may decide to team-teach as they address the whole class. The most important part of this workshop structure is that the students are given the opportunity to take charge of their learning to the greatest extent possible. During the "You Do!" stage, teachers may meet with individual students or in small groups, or utilize this time as valuable formative assessment to monitor students' performance.

Note that the time for the students to apply (You Do!) should take up most of the instructional time. The principles of UDL connect seamlessly with this workshop model. Learners are engaged, active learners who apply strategic thinking as they learn to monitor their understanding and progress. Learning is not about completing tasks to simply comply with teacher directions. It becomes about students' making sense of the content and materials and processing the information at their own pace and level of understanding. The workshop structure provides opportunities for students to connect to learning that goes beyond simply connecting to tasks to complete. Since most of the instructional time allows for high levels of student voice and application, the learning becomes an authentic process.

## STRATEGIES TO MAINTAIN HIGH EXPECTATIONS

In Chapter 3, we discussed Edwin Ellis's *Watering Up the Curriculum* (1999). The concepts are worth revisiting here because Ellis's model can help ensure that co-teachers apply scaffolds and accommodations in ways that maintain high expectations for all learners. We know that the variability of all learners can be supported through instruction that has strong scaffolds to guide students to connect meaningfully with the content. The better learners connect the content with their own background knowledge, the more they will learn and remember.

When connected to the UDL Guidelines, Ellis's nine goals provide additional guidance for teachers to involve learners as allies in implementing UDL. In addition, these nine goals connect seamlessly to the UDL principles and guidelines. I offer a start to your thinking by including a UDL connection to spark your continued applications.

1.  **More emphasis on students constructing knowledge**

    Teachers facilitate learning to allow students to seek information, process it, and express their understandings. Students have opportunities to connect previously learned information with new information.

    **The UDL Connection:**

    Consider multiple means of action and expression. Offer multiple tools and strategy to use. Vary the methods of response to allow each learner to connect and express her expanded knowledge in meaningful ways.

2. **More depth, less superficial coverage**

   Teachers deliver learning experiences that allow students to process ideas and understand why they are important and how they connect. Teachers make time to experience learning with students rather than just covering the information based on what is written in their plan book or curriculum guide.

   **The UDL Connection:**

   Consider multiple means of representation to allow students to perceive information in welcoming, familiar, and exciting ways. Once students make that first meaningful step, move the lesson into an active process where they are actively thinking, speaking, sharing, and learning.

3. **More emphasis on developing relational understanding and knowledge connections**

   As a way to guide deeper understandings, teachers provide students with the opportunity to see how ideas and concepts are connected. Information is taught within a context of what a student knows to allow him to associate new learning with known information.

   **The UDL Connection:**

   Consider multiple means of engagement. How can you optimize relevance, value, and authenticity as you connect your goals, content, and materials with the strengths and needs of your students? Be a keen observer so that you may read and understand how to guide each learner. Guide learners through multiple means of action and expression to connect new learning with previously taught information.

4. **More student elaboration**

   Include many opportunities for students to not only hear their own thoughts, but to share their voice. Cooperative learning, such as think-pair-share, provides valuable processing time for students to gain deeper understandings as well as confidence in their abilities.

   **The UDL Connection:**

   Consider multiple means of action and expression as you support strategy development.

5. **More emphasis on the redundancy of archetype concepts, patterns, and strategies**

Teachers facilitate learning in ways that help learners to see connections, repetition, and associations to guide their understanding and memory for important information. For example, students are taught themes of geography to improve their understanding when learning about ancient civilizations.

### The UDL Connection:

Consider multiple means of representation as you introduce new ideas. Including visuals and multimedia options through multiple means of action and expression will get students to see and experience the connections and associations to guide deeper understanding and retention.

6. **More reflection and risk-taking**

Teachers incorporate time for students to think about how they feel about what they are learning. They experiment with strategies that guide their learning, and they are free to share their ideas within an environment where their thinking is valued.

### The UDL Connection:

Consider multiple means of engagement to foster a collaborative learning community where students reflect and self-regulate the application of specific strategies.

7. **More social support for achievement**

Create opportunities for learners to strengthen their own voice as they develop tolerance and understanding for the views of others. In inclusive classrooms, cooperative learning and peer interactions are ideal opportunities for all learners to take the lead in learning, as well as learn from their peers.

### The UDL Connection:

Consider multiple means of engagement as you nurture an environment where learners value their thinking and are comfortable sharing their voice with peers. As students share their views, they learn to value the perspective of their peers.

8. **More emphasis on developing habits of mind, thinking skills, and learning strategies**

Learners have ongoing opportunities to develop a growth mind-set as they push through challenges. In addition, they learn a variety of strategies to guide them to be successful.

**The UDL Connection:**

Consider multiple means of action and expression, along with engagement, as learners set goals, plan, and apply strategies that optimize learning and self-reflection.

9. **More emphasis on developing a sense of personal potency**

The individual thinking of variable learners is valued. Each learner is supported along a learning process that fosters interpersonal, intrapersonal, and academic success.

**The UDL Connection:**

Consider all three UDL principles. Multiple means of engagement will connect learners with goals and self-reflection. Multiple means of representation will allow each learner to maximize personal connections and transfer of material. Multiple means of action and expression will support strategic, goal-directed learners.

Co-teachers should combine their efforts and expertise as they combine the co-teaching models, UDL principles, and watering-up goals.

# GENERAL TIPS FOR EFFECTIVE SCAFFOLDING

1. Identify what the students need to know and be able to do.

   - Consider the lesson you will be teaching and decide on the background students will need to know.

   - Identify any barriers in the way between students' current performance levels and the desired achievement.

2. Begin with students' abilities.

   • Create learning experiences that balance students' feeling successful and students feeling motivated to complete more-complex tasks.

3. Guide students in frustration-free style.

   • Keep the learning target in mind and provide scaffolds toward achieving that target. For example, if the learning target is to have students gain and express knowledge of historical facts and write an essay, provide opportunities for learning along the way. For instance, incorporate opportunities that represent the material through multimedia formats to give students additional examples to perceive the information. In addition, create space for students to engage in discussions, and/or choice to sketch ideas, or jot ideas in an outline format to express their understanding of the historical facts before they are expected to write the essay.

4. Create a true learning community.

   • Individuality is honored and respected.

   • Everyone has an opportunity to share her voice.

5. Monitor and celebrate small successes.

   • Know when to nudge learners forward and when to release to see what they are able to do. Limit frustration and maximize success, and you will naturally motivate students to want to learn more.

6. Guide students to take charge of their learning.

   • Gradually release responsibility to the students.

   • Create natural self-monitoring opportunities.

   • Maximize opportunities to learn and practice executive functioning skills and strategies throughout each day.

# TAKEAWAY IDEAS

- UDL can be easily embedded within your daily classroom routines, structures, instructional decisions, and overall attitude for learning. As this happens, not only do learners want to learn, they also want to know *how* to learn.

- Co-teachers can set the tone by making intentional decisions to incorporate time for students to embrace struggling as a natural part of the learning process. UDL empowers teachers to optimize opportunities for students to learn from mistakes and become motivated to improve and continue to learn and share ideas.

- As teachers expose students to the language of the UDL principles and planned activities, students experience the opportunity to self-regulate and to take charge of their personal learning process. Through specific discussions, activities, and lessons, students begin to deepen their awareness about who they are as learners.

- Remember, our goal as educators is to create expert learners. That means we must value the thinking and the learning process of each learner. Each learner must have the opportunity to not only access the curriculum, but to experience the content in ways that deepen his or her relationship with learning.

- With two teachers in the room, co-teachers can maximize learning by incorporating the talents of both teachers through varied co-teaching models, UDL strategies, and specially designed instruction, as needed. Maintain high expectations for all learners by incorporating the specific goals of watering up the curriculum to elevate student voice, choice, and engaged learning experiences.

# STUDY GROUP QUESTIONS

1. Share one way you create a risk-free learning environment with your co-teacher and students. How do you make sure that each learner in the room is comfortable with being a part of the learning process?

2. When thinking about introducing your students to UDL, what is one idea that you feel would work with your students? What ideas does your co-teacher have?

3. How do the UDL Guidelines and the goals of watering up the curriculum by Edwin Ellis naturally unite to empower your instructional decisions?

4. Share a recent experience that you feel demonstrates evidence of UDL principles in your classroom.

5. Share one lesson objective—what is an example of a scaffold you incorporated to guide one or more students to achieve the objective? What UDL principle or guideline aligns with your example? How is your example connected to Ellis's model of watering up the curriculum?

6. Finish this sentence: I know I am in a UDL classroom when. . .

# More Strategies and Structures to Promote Learner Expertise

7

THE UDL GUIDELINES OFFER POWERFUL AND SPECIFIC STRATEGIES TO HELP US ENGAGE LEARNERS AND HELP THEM BECOME SELF-EMPOWERED, EXPERT LEARNERS. As we weave in multiple ways of action and expression, we touch upon multiple ways of representing materials to meet the needs of the variability in our classrooms. The strategies shared in this book may elevate the instructional process as two teachers join forces to make meaningful learning happen.

The strategies outlined in this chapter provide a sampling of effective ways to help the learners in your room become *expert* learners—that is, learners who are purposeful and resourceful, who know where to seek resources, and who they can go to with questions and comments to seek more information (CAST, 2011). They become motivated and knowledgeable by setting goals and applying strategies that guide their thinking and confidence to be the absolute best version of themselves as possible. These strategies will help you as co-teachers:

- Eliminate a sense of threat and create a comfortable learner-centered environment.

- Facilitate complex, meaningful, real-world thinking.

- Respect the uniqueness of each learner.

- Provide peer support and specific feedback.

- Encourage self-monitoring and reflection as connected to learning goals.

- Promote active, relevant, choice-driven learning.

Expert learners know *how* to learn—not just in a particular class but everywhere they go.

As we know, our structural decisions are not enough. We must make sure that any co-teaching model and any teaching structure we apply is the frame for solid strategic and deep thinking through carefully designed instruction. Let's consider specific strategies that can make any classroom illuminate with UDL. All strategies shared here may be effective for all grades and all content areas.

# STRATEGIES FOR PROVIDING OPTIONS FOR STUDENT CHOICE

The following strategies provide examples to keep students engaged, in control, and at the center of a meaningful learning process each day.

## Choose Own Seats

This is a simple, yet powerful, way to empower learners. When teachers assign seats for students, then that's saying to students, *I know what is best for you—and it doesn't matter if you think differently—I am the teacher and will make this decision.* Yet when students are given the options for seating, it can boost attention, behavior, and overall engagement. In the event that a student selects a seat that serves to distract himself and others from learning, you can use that as a teachable moment—or moments! You mention to the student that you notice he is distracted, and then ask him if he needs your help to guide better choices.

> **The UDL Connection:**
>
> **Engagement:** Students are empowered by their ability to choose, their choice to attend, and their ability to self-monitor their learning behaviors. These choices can minimize distractions and optimize motivation.
>
> **Action and Expression:** The process of peer collaboration and strategy development can be amplified through peer-to-peer interactions and flexible small groups during instructional time.
>
> **Co-teaching Tips:** Students can be allowed to sit anywhere they like, if the context of the lesson lends to this level of flexibility. Seating can be

considered flexible as students move their desks and chairs according to the lesson and the day. There are two teachers, so the monitoring to ensure success is doubled. Clock Buddies (for elementary) and Assignment Buddies (for upper elementary and secondary) are also effective. Learn more at www.readingquest.org/strat/clock_buddies.html.

# Choice Boards

Choice boards are menus of activities that provide multiple options for students to explore and deepen their understanding on a given topic or concept. It is effective in all content areas, including math, science, social studies, and English. When creating choice boards, teachers should consider the learning goal and key concepts for understanding. As choices are planned, make sure the key concepts and goals drive the activity options you develop. It is critical to connect the activity with the assessment of students' understanding and achievement toward the learning goal.

The UDL Connection:

**Engagement:** The option to select activities increases motivation and optimizes autonomy. Students are easily focused on the goals and objectives by participating in meaningful activities. Students have the opportunity to take charge of their learning and work at their own pace.

**Representation:** Each activity may offer a variety of presentation modes. For example, one activity may link to a video and then ask students to reflect on the content. Another activity may offer the opportunity to analyze song lyrics or a graph or any visual that connects to the subject and concept.

**Action and Expression:** Each activity provides a different way to express one's understanding. For example, one activity may ask students to compose a song to describe a turning point in history or a section of a piece of literature. Another activity can ask students to write, act, create a podcast, design a poster, or write a poem to express knowledge and understanding.

**Co-teaching Tips:** The power of two teachers to create activity options will highlight each other's area of expertise. One co-teacher may be savvy with technology, whereas the other is more artistic. The point is to combine the greatness each teacher has to offer. There is so much to learn from each other, as well.

# Choice of Assessment

When developing classroom assessments to determine a student's understanding of completed units of study, teachers typically give one test to all students. Why not offer a test where you provide a few options for demonstrating their understanding? Allow students to choose between writing, speaking, and creating as a means of expressing any given concept. The key is to plan out your style of assessment over time to allow for an appropriate balance of developing the ability to gain knowledge and in responding to various types of assessment. For example, students should have practice with multiple-choice and essay questions, but that should not be the only style of assessment when considering learning through a UDL lens.

In addition, consider the voice of self-assessment as a tool for preparing students for an upcoming summative assessment. Prepare review sheets that guide students to code their level of understanding and prepare their focus for study.

### The UDL Connection:

**Engagement:** The opportunity for self-assessment creates a meaningful process for students reflect and connect with themselves as learners. Students gain a strong grasp on what they know and what they need to work on; they own their learning by persevering through challenges and celebrating their personal achievements.

**Action and Expression:** Students are given the opportunity to respond using varied methods.

**Co-teaching Tips:** Combine ideas for allowing the content and skills of your class to align with individual students' strengths and abilities. Meet the students where they are by coming together to plan your assessment procedures and formats. In addition, if the general education teacher plans an assessment, she should share it with the special education teacher, so that individual has plenty of time to review and add any UDL ideas—for example, perhaps a simple change in font size, formatting to include more space between questions, or more substantial changes that the teachers feel are appropriate. Both teachers should maintain the same high expectations for all learners.

# Brainstorming Breaks

No matter what grade or subject you teach, make time for students to process. All learners need some time to take in the information that is presented. Allow time for students to reflect on segments of your lesson individually by jotting down their comments or questions in their notebooks. Another option is to strategically place chart paper around the room. Make time for a two- to four-minute pause for students to get up out of their seats and write down their thoughts on the paper. The students may then take another two minutes to discuss their thinking in these small groups. These choices for brainstorming allow all students to participate, compared to just brainstorming with the whole class where only a few students share.

### The UDL Connection:

**Engagement:** All students have the opportunity to develop self-reflection skills rather than getting lost in the mix of a whole-class lesson where they too easily fall into the "let someone else participate" mode. This flexible brainstorming method fosters collaboration and increases the level of building a community of learners.

**Representation:** Students are exposed to the thinking of others through movement and written and oral expression. Students may also have the option to sketch their thoughts on the chart paper rather than write them down in words.

**Action and Expression:** The movement between listening, note-taking, and reflecting keeps learners alert and attentive. This reflective brainstorming and cooperative group learning strengthens learners' ability to monitor their understanding and increases their ability to communicate what they know and what they still wonder about.

**Co-teaching Tips:** The management piece is always an added bonus for strategies that require movement and monitoring. Since minimal to no preparation is involved, co-teachers can plan ahead or decide in the moments of teaching that this is a great way to keep learners engaged and learning.

## Student Inquiry Teams

Setting up the structure for student inquiry teams takes a bit of planning, but it is a great way to provide choice and increase learning in any classroom. All you need to do is connect the subject area you teach with a few open-ended questions that would spark students' problem-solving and fact-finding skills.

It could be math equations or word problems, or it could be a question to support the themes and concepts in any content area classroom. It is a great way to incorporate research skills, as well.

### The UDL Connection:

**Engagement:** Providing a choice between questions for inquiry optimizes autonomy and motivation. The process of inquiry should wrap around clear goals for learning.

**Representation:** There are many ways teachers can introduce and support the process of these inquiry-based projects. Students may select from a list of teacher-generated questions. Teachers may provide students with links to take them to the class website or videos that spark the learning process.

**Action and Expression:** This peer-collaborative activity is deeply seated in choices. Students may be allowed to choose their teams. Or even if the teams are teacher-selected, students have decisions to make as they direct their solution-seeking mind-sets into action. Teachers can keep a stack of resources on tables around the room so students can access these books and articles. Teachers can arrange for guest speakers to come and address some of the topics. And of course, technology such as iPads, Chromebooks, or desktop computers, provides boundless digital, multimedia resources. Check with your school librarian, who will be a wealth of information and ideas.

**Co-teaching Tips:** Students may gain further motivation by also creating their own questions to direct their learning. Consider providing the option for students to generate their ideas based on the concepts and topic of your class. An additional consideration may be to provide the choice for students to go solo. It is not always necessary to force collaboration when we are guiding learners. A healthy balance is key—especially for learners who have specific goals for working individually and in groups.

# Hint Cards

This low-prep strategy guides metacognition and self-regulation. Hint cards encourage students to take control of their learning in real time. Oftentimes when students are asked to work independently, they struggle quietly or just sit unproductively until class time is over. Hint cards make supports available to all learners in the room. Students learn to self-regulate and ask deeper questions to guide their own learning.

Teachers decide on the challenging points in a learning activity where students may need additional support. It may be that students need a review of definitions or examples of previously taught concepts or vocabulary words. In math, hint cards can also include sample problems worked out step by step, so students can deepen their understanding of the mathematical thinking they need to apply to their work. The hint cards are placed strategically around the room.

### The UDL Connection:

**Engagement:** The threat of singling struggling learners out of the group is minimized as the option is offered to all learners. As students choose to review the various hint cards, they may opt to discuss with peers to further their understanding. The movement around the room as students select the level of support they need optimizes motivation and a focus on learning goals.

**Representation:** Hint cards can be handwritten or typed printed cards. Teachers may also provide iPads or Chromebooks with a link for students to watch a video or view a website that may serve as a scaffold/hint to trigger deeper understanding and application.

**Action and Expression:** Hint cards can be prepared using multiple tools and technologies. Students build their fluency of knowledge at graduated levels of supports as they choose the hints they feel support their personal achievements.

**Co-teaching Tips:** This is a clear way to provide specific supports without singling any student out of the crowd. Students make the choice to use the hints as they see their peers use them and/or as they see the hints are offered to anyone who would like to use them. Co-teachers may need to coach the class and/or specific students with a gentle reminder that the hints are there and just waiting to be used. The Teaching Channel has a helpful video to see it in action: https://www.teachingchannel.org/videos/hint-cards.

# Flex-Time

There is something just so powerful about allowing students the freedom to use a specific amount of time in any way they choose—as long as it supports the learning that has been going on in class. Depending on the grade and subject, flex-time is a great addition to class routines on a weekly or monthly basis. Students have the opportunity to empower their relationship with learning by selecting a specific task to practice or learn more about.

### The UDL Connection:

**Engagement:** This time is ideal for promoting personal strategic thinking. Learners decide how best to use this time as they expand their strategy applications and skills. Teachers may provide specific feedback to support students' mastery of specific goals.

**Representation:** Make a variety of tools and technologies available depending on your resources and on the specific tasks.

**Action and Expression:** Students work independently to build their knowledge and strategy base. This is an opportunity to optimize access to tools and technologies as appropriate for your resources and tasks for this time.

**Co-teaching Tips:** This flex-time option optimizes any reteaching or explicit instruction that is needed for students with specific IEP goals. Both teachers should optimize this time to connect with students on their path to becoming expert learners. This is a perfect time for teachers to gain valuable formative assessment feedback on student performance.

# SUPPORTING CONTENT-AREA READING, WRITING, LISTENING, AND SPEAKING

The following strategies provide examples to guide learners to develop strategic thinking as they deepen their long-term connection with their learning process.

## SQRW (Scan–Question–Read–Write)

The SQRW strategy (Strichart & Mangrum, 2002) naturally allows learners to follow the steps of effective reading by following four simple manageable steps. Teachers can model and gradually release responsibility for students to be able to:

- **Scan** the text by noticing the text features, such as images, captions, titles, subtitles, bold print, and so on. This step allows students to get ready to comprehend by previewing key features and connecting to what they already know.

- **Question:** Using each subtitle, the student selects one question word—*who, what, where, when, why, how*—and changes the subtitle into a question. The student structures his notepaper using a Q&A fashion.

- **Read:** Once the question is written down, the student is ready to read that section of the text with intention and purpose.

- **Write:** As the student identifies the response to the question, he writes it down and gets ready to write the question for the next section of reading.

The UDL Connection:

**Engagement:** This strategy heightens the salience of the goals by having the student set a purpose and direct her reading comprehension throughout the reading time.

**Representation:** This strategy enhances textbook reading. It is also ideal when reading digital texts.

**Action and Expression:** Students have the option to write their notes in their notebooks, type their notes using technology, or work with a peer and take turns, with one peer being the speaker and the other writing down the notes.

# Reciprocal Teaching

Reciprocal teaching (Palincsar & Brown, 1984) can transform any reading activity, by guiding students to apply four active reading strategies: making predictions, asking questions, clarifying confusing words or phrases, and summarizing sections of the text. This strategy works well with literature and expository text and can be used in any grade. The teacher models reading a text by first making a prediction, and then continues to model her thinking as she questions, clarifies, and summarizes at various points in the text to demonstrate the natural flow and thinking during effective reading comprehension. The teacher moves to gradually release responsibility to the students as they practice with a peer. Students may take turns leading the group by facilitating the discussion at various points of the reading. These group leaders determine the section of reading that the students will complete. For example, the leaders says, "OK, everyone read to the bottom of page X." The leader continues to lead the group with questions at strategic points of the reading. He asks, "Who has a prediction? What questions do you have so far? Are there any confusing words or parts in the reading? Who wants to summarize what we read so far?" Students take turns being the leader (or teacher).

**The UDL Connection:**

**Engagement:** This strategy encourages students to develop self-assessment of their reading and comprehension skills. In addition, they practice pushing through challenges as they realize that all readers get confused at points and that clarifying is part of the reading process for all readers. In addition, the group work fosters collaboration and community.

**Representation:** The text that students read can be presented in books, articles, or digital form. In addition, text-to-speech programs can be used if appropriate. Strategy cards can be labeled Predict, Clarify, Question, Summarize, to serve as a visual and manipulative tool for students to stay focused on the strategies. The strategies can also be presented on the SMART Board or as PowerPoint slide, anchor charts, or individual student bookmarks.

**Action and Expression:** Strategy development and goal-setting are supported through the natural reciprocal-teaching reading process. Students' ability to self-monitor their comprehension is naturally embedded. In addition, multiple tools for students to respond can be incorporated through oral expression, written expression, and use of technology.

# Collaborative Strategic Reading

CSR (Klingner & Vaughn, 1999) is an effective strategy when guiding students to read content-area materials. The reading process involves four steps:

1. Preview: Students glance over text features to get an idea of what they are going to read as they connect to what they already know.

2. Click and clunk: Students work together to share what words and ideas they understood as key ideas (click) and what ideas or words they found confusing (clunk).

3. Get the gist: Students collaborate to summarize key points and paraphrase main ideas. In addition, they share why these ideas are important (the gist).

4. Wrap-up: After finishing the reading of all segments of the text, students summarize what they learned.

**The UDL Connection:**

**Engagement:** Collaboration and community are fostered through group discussions.

**Representation:** Text may be in the form of textbooks, articles, or digital format. Cue cards for the four steps should be presented as a visual scaffold.

**Action and Expression:** Students focus on strategic thinking and self-monitoring. In addition, they build fluency and stamina to deepen their ability to read more complex texts. Multiple media such as speech-to-text or text-to-speech options can be incorporated.

**Co-teaching Tips:** Consider the strengths of your students and assign a role to specific individuals to guide other students to take a leadership role in this reading group process. Make sure to scaffold the reading and writing process to knock down any barriers that prevent students from accessing and participating in this learning experience.

# Interactive Notebooks

This strategy teaches students to take any class lesson, concept, or lecture and transform the key points into meaningful notes and learning opportunities. Each student has a notebook dedicated to a specific subject area (math, science, social studies, English, study skills). Students use the right side of the notebook to glue the class notes from any particular day. The left side is for students to respond to those class notes. The idea is to give students time to process important information or concept(s). Student may choose to paraphrase, sketch, transfer information to a graphic organizer, or some other way to deepen their understanding so that they connect and transfer the information.

**The UDL Connection:**

**Engagement:** Students make the choice for how they will express their understanding on the left side of the page. They reflect and self-assess to gain deeper understanding.

**Representation:** Although the class notes that go on the right side of the page will be in the form of text or graphics, the instruction that surrounds the notes may include multimedia representations.

**Action and Expression:** Students have the option to sketch, write, and engage in discussions as they decide how to express their understanding on the left side of the notebook.

**Co-teaching Tips:** It is easy to individualize the process of creating these notebooks. Be sure to encourage each learner to apply his area of strength and talent to creating his understandings. Include peer interactions to spark each learner to connect to his understanding. Peer interactions can be a powerful process for connecting the learning with the learner.

# QAD (Question–Answer–Detail)

The QAD strategy encourages students to organize the process of sifting through key ideas when reading, listening, and/or creating meaningful notes to remember important information. This three-column notes organizer guides students through a sequential thinking process as they expand their understanding on a given topic/concept. The questions may be teacher-generated to guide students' focus and inquiry, or teachers may decide to ask students to create the questions to provide the opportunity for higher-level thinking. Questions should be generated based on what teachers want students to know about a particular topic. Questions are the driving force as they direct students to listening or reading to locate the answer and gather details to extend their knowledge.

**The UDL Connection:**

**Engagement:** QAD promotes expectations and focused strategy use to guide attention and motivation.

**Representation:** Students are guided to process information by visualizing the QAD sequence to organize their thinking.

**Action and Expression:** Multimedia options can be used to generate the notes. As students respond to questions, they increase their ability to self-monitor their performance by finding text evidence to verify their responses.

**Co-teaching Tips:** You may scaffold the process by allowing students to work in pairs or in groups. You can include digital options such as typing or engaging with speech-to-text technologies.

# FQR (Fact, Question, Response)

FQR (Harvey & Goudvis, 2000) is a three-column note-taking strategy that provides a visual structure to guide students' comprehension and deeper understanding about the content. In the column labeled "Facts," students list a few important facts about the topic or concept that students are responsible for knowing. This could be in preparation for reading a text, listening to a lecture, or viewing a video. Next to each fact, in the "Question" column, students write down a question that comes to mind during the learning experience. Following the learning, students write a response to their question as it connects to the listed fact. The response should deepen their understanding of the fact by guiding students to pose a question and seek a meaningful response.

**The UDL Connection:**

**Engagement:** Learners set a purpose for their reading, listening, or viewing by formulating a question based on the selected fact.

**Representation:** Texts and/or technology can easily be incorporated to present the content. Access to the Internet can be an added way to present information through videos, podcasts, online images, and so forth.

**Action and Expression:** Teachers can design the process and products to allow students to write, speak, and sketch as they create facts, questions, and responses. In addition, cooperative groups can be formed to allow peers to assign roles to one another for speaking, researching, writing, and so forth.

**Co-teaching Tips:** If students are reading a text, you can provide the students with three differently colored sticky notes; for example, "Facts" written on blue stickies, "Questions" written on yellow stickies, and "Responses" written on yellow stickies. Students may place their stickies on a small-group or whole-class chart to allow students to learn from one another. In addition, teachers may want to begin with teacher-selected facts to guide a focus on specific knowledge their students need to have.

## Connect, Collect, Correct

Connect, collect, correct (Carreker, 2004) is a powerful three-column note-taking organizer that promotes strategic thinking and world knowledge by tapping into students' background knowledge prior to a reading, listening, or viewing exercise. Students jot down what they know about the topic/concept and then as they read, listen, or view the content, they record details about the topic. Students check for understanding during the moments of learning and add their new thinking in the "correct" column. I like to add "confirm" to the "collect" column when students' background knowledge and collection of details align with their new, expanded views. Students learn to integrate new information.

**The UDL Connection:**

**Engagement:** This strategy promotes active reading, listening, and speaking. In addition, teachers may incorporate peer/class discussions to incorporate collaboration.

**Representation:** Teachers have the flexibility to use digital presentations, text presentations, and audio modes of presenting information.

**Action and Expression:** Use of multiple means of media and communication are evident through thoughtful instructional design. Teachers have the flexibility to design learning around multiple tools for constructing knowledge.

**Co-teaching Tips:** Consider opening the lesson with a quick review through engaging video or other visuals along with class discussion to trigger background knowledge for students before having them write their initial connections.

# Card Pyramid

A card pyramid (Carreker, 2004) may be used to organize main idea and supporting details and facts through this visual scaffold to guide their oral or written summaries. This strategy has a lot of flexibility in the way teachers want to apply it. You can use index cards so students can move the cards around as a visual-kinesthetic reminder to keep them on track. You can also use colored felt squares that you prepare for students to use. For example, you may cut a blue square to symbolize the main idea, and yellow squares to indicate each detail that supports that main idea. Figure 7.1 shows another version where I covered cardboard blocks with paper to create a block pyramid and labeled them with "Main idea" and "Supporting detail" to guide fourth- and fifth-grade students to include three details to support the main idea of a text. This visual and kinesthetic scaffold guided the students' thinking. This block pyramid works well to include the visual and kinesthetic, as well as the added auditory, excitement of the blocks falling if the students' summary or explanation needed more organization and details. If the students did not include a strong main idea to support the details, the pyramid fell down and crashed, which caused them to smile and push through the challenge to build their thinking more clearly.

**The UDL Connection:**

**Engagement:** Students are focused on the goal of zooming in on main ideas and key details. Visuals and kinesthetic input scaffolds motivation and attention.

**Representation:** Teachers have the option to present information in ways where they maximize the use of available resources. The teachers' creative side has room to grow here.

**Action and Expression:** Options for multiple means of communication and knowledge building are left to the teachers' connection between resources and specific needs of students in class. Teachers have the opportunity to allow students to process and express ideas in ways that connect with their individual strengths.

**Co-teaching Tips:** Connect students' individual IEP goals with this activity to ensure heightened success with expressing main ideas and details. Consider peer interactions to support collaborative options.

**FIGURE 7.1.** Block pyramid

The block pyramid (Figure 7.1) is another version of the card pyramid strategy to guide students' oral and/or written expression to include clear, concise main ideas and details following reading or listening to a text or lesson.

# Concept Circles

Concept circles (Vacca & Vacca, 1986) are a quick, easy-to-implement visual for remembering key vocabulary words that expand students' understanding of important concepts and themes. Each concept circle has a heading to indicate the concept, and then students add the vocabulary words to demonstrate deeper understanding as they expand their vocabulary. See Figure 7.2 for a sample concept circle around the Westward Expansion. Students may add sketches and words next to, or on the back of, the concept circle to add details to this great visual and study guide.

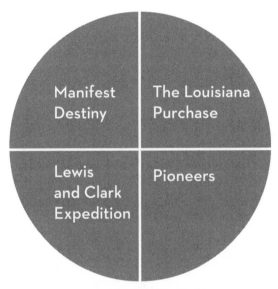

**FIGURE 7.2.** Sample of a concept circle for the Westward Expansion

The UDL Connection:

**Engagement:** Vary the demands and resources for students as they complete the concept circles to optimize attention and motivation.

**Representation:** A variety of texts, videos, website links, podcasts, and so forth may be set up for students to explore and build their background knowledge and review of the concept.

**Action and Expression:** An additional way to apply concept circles is by having students fill in the concept circles based on their class notes and background knowledge base only. This introduces the additional process of self-monitoring what they know in preparation for a summative or formative assessment. They may then evaluate what they know and expand their knowledge by seeking available multimedia resources.

**Co-teaching Tips:** Be sure to provide explicit small-group instruction to instill the importance and process of selecting key words. Oftentimes, students have difficulty determining what is most important to remember. Guide the process and release the responsibility to them as they are ready, and be a keen observer and listener to what they do and say!

# Exclusion Brainstorming

Exclusion brainstorming (Blachowicz, 1986) is an effective way to create student-led discussions and critical thinking skills. The teacher presents a word cloud or list of words related to a given topic or concept. Students work as a team, in small groups, or as a whole class to decide what words should be eliminated because they do not capture the essence of the main topic. This strategic process encourages students to evaluate the facts and their understanding. Students must justify their thinking as they decide to keep or eliminate listed words. This process guides learners to determine importance while learning.

### The UDL Connection:

**Engagement:** Strategic thinking is encouraged as students are given the choice to decide what words to eliminate, and then asked to justify and explain their thinking.

**Representation:** Digital tools such as Wordle (www.wordle.net), teacher-created PowerPoint or SMART Board slides, and so forth can be used. In addition, good old-fashioned markers and chart paper can be a good way to go.

**Action and Expression:** Students become engaged in a process of collaboration by calling out answers, and deleting or crossing words off the list on the board. Students' listening and speaking skills are highlighted to extend strategy development and communication.

**Co-teaching Tips:** Consider giving students individual copies of the words so that they may physically cross out words as the learning unfolds, thus providing an added personal visual as well.

# STRATEGIES FOR PEER COLLABORATION WITH FOCUS ON LISTENING AND SPEAKING

The following strategies provide opportunities for fostering a sense of community as the UDL principles are naturally embedded to bridge a clear path between the content and each learner in the classroom.

## Accountable Talk

Build a community of learners by providing students with opportunities to use their natural inclination to speak with one another. Students will process information more deeply through active discussion as they listen to the thoughts of others and justify their own thinking. Students respond to and add their thinking to what others in the group have said. They discuss relevant and accurate knowledge based on the topic and content the teachers design. Students are active, attentive listeners who use evidence from a text or source of information to support their thinking. Here are ways students learn during these conversations:

- Paraphrasing or repeating to clarify what others have said (known as re-voicing)

- Adding to someone else's thinking

- Explaining their reasoning

- Posing challenging questions to dig deeper into topics for discussion

**Example of Conversation Stems:**

I wonder about. . .

I would like to add to what _____ was saying.

Could you please clarify/explain what you mean?

At first I thought _____, but now I think _____.

After reading _____, I came to the conclusion that _____.

I agree/disagree because _____.

Your thinking connects with mine because I think _____.

## The UDL Connection:

**Engagement:** Accountable talk fosters collaboration and community as it develops students' self-reflection. Students provide feedback to one another as they share their thinking. Teachers also contribute to deepen the richness of discussions as needed.

**Representation:** Student conversations, as well as the conversation stems, make a perfect anchor chart for the classroom. In addition, you may decide to make it a digital slide and present it as needed. You can give students topics/questions for discussion after they view a video, navigate a website and digital text, or read a book, an article, or information listed on index cards.

**Action and Expression:** Listening and speaking are encouraged with this strategy, yet students may have additional methods as options for communication. For example, you can have one student take the minutes and type or write down the conversation to be used for future studying and discussion.

**Co-teaching Tips:** Remember the value of UDL and additional scaffolds through SDI; make sure that each group has the right amount of challenge along with supports to master communication skills as they gain meaningful knowledge on the topic of discussion. Each group, and each student in each group, does not have to be doing the same thing.

# Lansdown Word Cards

Sharon Lansdown (1991) designed this strategy as a way to actively involve her students in remembering key ideas and vocabulary during a lesson. Here's one way to apply the strategy:

1. Teacher(s) determine the topic of the lesson and prepare index cards, with one key vocabulary word per card.

2. Each student receives a card and is asked to hold up his or her card as the word is spoken during the lesson.

3. As the students hold up their cards, the teacher may decide to pause to discuss the term in the context of the lesson and overall concept.

Students learn vocabulary in context, as well as gain active listening skills and increased background knowledge.

### The UDL Connection:

**Engagement:** This strategy fosters a sense of community as students look around to see who is holding up word cards and then participating in class discussions.

**Representation:** Word cards may be presented with graphics and images to extend the students' understanding.

**Action and Expression:** Listening and speaking are highly encouraged to strengthen students' communication skills. The use of technology to extend class discussions can deepen the experience as students learn new ideas and concepts. Students may spend time in peer collaborations matching definitions of words with the context sentences to illustrate the meaning of words for greater retention. Words are selected from content area subjects and/or literature.

**Co-teaching Tips:** Peer tutoring can be used to increase motivation and student understanding. As words are raised, allow time for students to discuss the meaning of each word within the context of the lesson. You may differentiate the complexity of the words given to students by strategically handing out the word cards.

## Text on Text

Groups of three to five students gather around one large-print copy of a text. Each student uses a different color of marker to write comments, connections, or questions based on his or her reading of the text. Students may respond to one another's comments, as well. Then, the whole class joins in a gallery walk (see the Gallery Walk strategy a bit later) to read and write comments generated by other groups. Oral discussions may also occur in groups or as a whole class. See Figure 7.3 and Figure 7.4.

### The UDL Connection:

**Engagement:** This strategy fosters a strong sense of collaboration and community as students share and learn about one another's perspectives. Options for self-regulation are naturally embedded as students decide what to share through their collaborations. They also extend their thinking by adding on to peers' comments, which optimizes motivation.

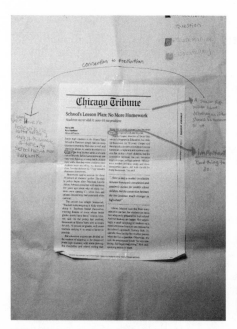

**FIGURE 7.3.** Student active reading sample

**FIGURE 7.4.** Collaborative annotations

**Representation:** You can spur creativity by presenting texts on poster paper with colorful markers. You can also present text on Chromebooks or iPads, and students can use speech-to-text technology to document their thinking.

**Action and Expression:** The process of this collaboration is typically through written discussions until later on when all comments have been added. Teachers may decide to include oral expression throughout the process if it is in the best interest of students' needs. In addition, students can be encouraged to sketch their ideas, so invite them to draw.

**Co-teaching Tips:** It is a good idea to model the process of this strategy. Co-teachers may demonstrate how it is done, and then hang up their finished product as a model and visual scaffold for students.

In Figure 7.3, these seventh-grade students decided to provide a key for active reading to guide their thinking (see the upper-right corner). They provided their own additional scaffold, which is evidence of effective self-monitoring and reflection. Talk about engagement!

In Figure 7.4, students engage in written text on text. Collaborative annotations deepen readers' thinking by providing time for them to think about their understanding of the topic then share their thinking through written expression. Students are free to jot down words, sketches, phrases, or sentences. In this figure, these students reflect on identifying the main idea—along with making time to express how collaborative annotation is helping them to better comprehend the text.

## Corners: Get Up and Go

With this strategy, students have the opportunity to get up and move around, and ponder the topic/concept presented by the teacher(s). Teachers present an open-ended question or statement that is based on the unit of study. Once they settle on the question, they decide on the degrees of agreement/disagreement and post each on a card around the room. For example, let's think about the question "Should we celebrate Christopher Columbus?" The degrees of agreement/disagreement could be "Yes, absolutely!," "Maybe," "Definitely not!," and "Not sure yet. . . I am still thinking about that." Students then move to the corner of the room that states how they feel. As students move into their groups, teachers give students a few minutes to discuss what they feel—and why they feel that way. The activity ends as the whole class comes together to share the main discussions from each group. Teachers can also opt to have students write down their responses in addition to speaking with peers.

### The UDL Connection:

**Engagement:** Learning is stimulated through movement, which can keep learners more alert and motivated. Peer interactions foster a sense of collaboration as learners gain a stronger sense of autonomy and develop personal opinions based on facts.

**Representation:** Providing students this time to think more deeply about a topic or concept maximizes transfer and deeper understandings. Visual scaffolds such as videos, graphics, illustrations, and texts can be offered to guide information processing and synthesizing.

**Action and Expression:** Students' listening, oral communication, critical thinking, and decision-making are highlighted. The integration of movement to a specific section of the room provides a voice for those students who may not be ready to speak out loud. Students can also be given the option to record their discussions and play them back for the whole class to listen to and discuss further.

**Co-teaching Tips:** Clarify and review any vocabulary with visual scaffolds or a quick review before you have the students move to their group.

## Points to Ponder

Let's face it; there are times when students just need to listen to a lecture, a video, a conversation, or any chunks of information. It is important for teachers to remember to stop and pause at strategic points to allow students to process and attach meaning to the information. At these stop points the teacher(s) should model the "points to ponder." What are those key points that need further thinking and clarification? Share out loud and create a list of these points to guide students' thinking.

**The UDL Connection:**

**Engagement:** Information is provided within a reasonable amount of time to maximize processing and retention, which easily facilitates coping and strategy skill development. Students' sense of community will come into play in this relaxed, stimulating learning environment.

**Representation:** Information can be represented in ways that suit the subject and specific style of the teacher, students, and resources available.

As the information is presented (with the idea that multimedia maximizes presenting information in ways to meet all learners in the context of the lesson), students have time to clarify vocabulary and concepts during the stop points as the teacher guides deeper awareness to encourage students to ponder and think more deeply.

**Action and Expression:** Students deepen their understanding by listening to the teachers' think-aloud. Students can work in pairs, small groups, or solo as they decide what points are important to ponder at that point of the lesson. In addition, this points-to-ponder time provides students with the opportunities to self-monitor their progress and understanding. You may even decide to have students jot down their points as added written expression or sketch their ideas to document their thinking.

**Co-teaching Tips:** You can plan ahead for some or all of the stop points, but be flexible in the moments as you notice how your students are responding. Adjust stop points, as needed.

## Peer-to-Peer Think-aloud

Sometimes students need time to think about the information without teachers getting in the way! Here's a way to break up lectures or longer segments of any lesson. Stop every so often to allow your students to process how they connect the lesson with their background knowledge. Allow students to do one of two ideas (their choice!):

1. Repeat an important fact or idea that you just heard, and share how it connects to something you already know.

2. Pose a question: What is confusing you at this point in the lesson?

Give students a few minutes to share with one another. If questions arise and students still need clarifications, either make time to respond right then and there or collect students' questions and be sure to catch up with the students after class.

**The UDL Connection:**

**Engagement:** This strategy guides students to develop a sense of reflection. They begin to value and trust their instincts. They become eager to ask questions and to advocate for themselves as learners when they are given the time and space to exercise this right.

**Representation:** Always think in terms of providing options for auditory and visual information. Seek out available resources that will match the context of each specific lesson.

**Action and Expression:** Providing this time for students to collaborate and process and synthesize the content with their own thinking allows for graduated levels of support and practice as students are given this time to think—really think.

**Co-teaching Tips:** Co-teachers should monitor the discussions with the pairs of students but should not interject or get involved unless they see students need guidance to get on a clear thinking path. Peer-to-peer think-aloud and interaction time can be valuable learning and leading time as students build confidence to process and share their thinking.

# Paraphrasing Ticket

Any content-area subject requires students to remember and communicate key academic vocabulary words to demonstrate their knowledge. Making time for students to express what they learned in their own words is one of the most empowering strategies. Students become confident in expressing their ideas, the facts, their questions, and their beliefs when they are given additional practice to articulate their thoughts out loud and in writing. Make time for students to complete a paraphrase ticket at the end of a lesson, at the end of class, or any time you feel it is appropriate to guide their academic communications.

### The UDL Connection:

**Engagement:** Making the time to paraphrase key understandings highlights the goals and objectives of any lesson. In addition, students begin to develop deeper reflections and self-assessment within the process of any lesson because they become comfortable with putting facts and concepts into their own words.

**Representation:** Think multimedia. Think about your available resources. Think about how you can present your lesson in a way that supports students' background knowledge and processing of important information.

**Action and Expression:** This is a great way to increase students' written expression because these are short, quick writings where students gain practice within a relaxed environment.

**Co-teaching Tips:** Vary the methods of response, as needed. Students may sketch, verbalize, or act out any concepts as they paraphrase key points.

## Gallery Walk

A gallery walk is a great way to get students up and moving as they gain knowledge and communication skills in any class or lesson. Teacher(s) share an open-ended question or statement with students. Students work in groups to respond to this question by creating a group poster. Once each group has completed their poster, they hang it up or place in on a table around the room. The class then circulates around the room so each group may explore and learn from one another. A spokesperson from each group may stay by his or her group's work to answer any questions or provide further details.

### The UDL Connection:

**Engagement:** Peer collaborations deepen a sense of community in the classroom. During the creation of the posters, students have a clear focus on the goals of the lesson, and they have the freedom of choice as they decide how to create their response.

**Representation:** The lesson that leads up to the gallery walk may be presented in a way that makes sense with meeting the needs of the learning objectives and the students. Academic vocabulary can be supported through anchor charts and the use of individual thesaurus books or apps on an iPad or Chromebook for students to clarify any vocabulary needed to create their poster.

**Action and Expression:** Students can use any media that the teacher(s) have available. Art supplies can be brought in for students to draw, paint, and illustrate their ideas. Chromebooks or iPads can be used for students to create a blog post, podcast, PowerPoint, or Prezi.

**Co-teaching Tips:** Monitor the flow of the movement and conversations to ensure maximum learning. You may opt to have students leave comments on a sticky note or on a sheet of paper to provide feedback to each group. Teachers, don't forget to leave your specific feedback to each group, as well.

## Learning Links

In small groups, students jot down their ideas to support an open-ended question or the task of summarizing key points of any given topic or subject. Each student jots down his or her idea and places it in the center of the table. The students spend time reading each others' ideas and decide how each response connects to the lesson or unit of study. Students create one thematic sentence to illustrate a central idea to their thinking.

### The UDL Connection:

**Engagement:** Students value their thinking and the thinking of their peers through meaningful discussions.

**Representation:** Students identify and build upon their background knowledge. Information processing is guided through shared written and oral expressions. Multimedia options may easily be incorporated to illustrate ideas in a variety of ways.

**Action and Expression:** Students can write on sticky notes, chart paper, sentence strips, or dry-erase boards. Digital tools such as Padlet (www.padlet.com) can be used to allow students to jot their ideas down on digital forum.

**Co-teaching Tips:** If you would like to focus on oral expression and an easily flowing conversation, then each group can select one "reporter" to write down student comments. Additionally, students can sketch their ideas and create captions to label their sketch for clarification purposes.

# Line-ups

The line-ups approach is a structured way to get students out of their seats and thinking on their feet. Simply line students up in two lines. Organize the lines in whatever way suits the physical space in your room (either next to each other or one line at the left side of the room and the other line at the right). One teacher stands at the front of the board and asks a question based on a recently taught subject matter. The teacher stands back and allows a student at the head of each line to take turns responding to the question. It may be posed in competition style if that serves to motivate and stimulate the learning—or each student from each line may collaborate to respond.

Once that question and its answer is discussed, students go to the end of the line and the next question—and next two students come up. Co-teachers take turns asking questions and monitoring students' attention. See Figure 7.5 for an example of how the line-up strategy was used in one fourth-grade class as the teachers provided additional time for the students to practice their multiplication facts.

### The UDL Connection:

**Engagement:** You can focus on collaboration and building knowledge and fluency of facts within a community of learners.

**Representation:** Material and content can be represented in a variety of formats. Teachers should select a method of representation that suits the specific lesson. For example, if this activity is implemented to review for an upcoming content area assessment, teachers can prepare index cards to read with a variety of questions to target the information the students need to know. Another way to present the material is through digital PowerPoint slides with questions and answers visually scaffolded for the students.

**Action and Expression:** Getting students up and out of their seats is always a good idea to keep them alert and as focused as possible. Students strengthen their oral and/or written expression communication skills as they participate in the planned activity.

**Co-teaching Tips:** Anchor charts can be used as visual scaffolds to trigger memory of key terms to scaffold accuracy and fluency. In addition, teachers should consider reminding students that they need to give one another "time to think" to allow wait time for students to process and respond with their best efforts and abilities.

**FIGURE 7.5.** Example of how the line-up approach was used in one fourth-grade classroom to practice multiplication facts

# TAKEAWAY IDEAS

- All classrooms—any subject, any grade—may elevate instruction by designing with UDL in mind. The UDL Guidelines provide a clear structure for teachers to apply specific strategies and structures to meet the needs of variable learners in the room.

- The co-teaching models are a structure for organizing groups of students to maximize learning. The models alone do not serve as an instructional strategy.

- Co-teachers must design all instruction within each lesson and each selected co-teaching model around the students' needs.

- In addition to the co-teaching models, co-teachers may consider the workshop structure that creates time for students to apply and transfer the knowledge and concepts they are learning in class. Any class instruction may be elevated with strategies that connect to UDL with keeping the learner at the center of meaningful learning experiences.

- Any class instruction may be elevated with strategies that connect to UDL with keeping the learner at the center of meaningful learning experiences.

# STUDY GROUP QUESTIONS

1. Name three strategies from this chapter that you would like to apply in your classroom.

2. Share two connections you made as you read through this chapter on structures and strategies.

3. Name one strategy from this chapter or from your own repertoire of strategies and explain how it can support the variable learners in your classroom. Use the UDL Guidelines (Figure 7.6) as a reference to support your thinking.

# Universal Design for Learning Guidelines

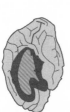

## Provide Multiple Means of Engagement
*Purposeful, motivated learners*

**Provide options for self-regulation**
+ Promote expectations and beliefs that optimize motivation
+ Facilitate personal coping skills and strategies
+ Develop self-assessment and reflection

**Provide options for sustaining effort and persistence**
+ Heighten salience of goals and objectives
+ Vary demands and resources to optimize challenge
+ Foster collaboration and community
+ Increase mastery-oriented feedback

**Provide options for recruiting interest**
+ Optimize individual choice and autonomy
+ Optimize relevance, value, and authenticity
+ Minimize threats and distractions

## Provide Multiple Means of Representation
*Resourceful, knowledgeable learners*

**Provide options for comprehension**
+ Activate or supply background knowledge
+ Highlight patterns, critical features, big ideas, and relationships
+ Guide information processing, visualization, and manipulation
+ Maximize transfer and generalization

**Provide options for language, mathematical expressions, and symbols**
+ Clarify vocabulary and symbols
+ Clarify syntax and structure
+ Support decoding of text, mathematical notation, and symbols
+ Promote understanding across languages
+ Illustrate through multiple media

**Provide options for perception**
+ Offer ways of customizing the display of information
+ Offer alternatives for auditory information
+ Offer alternatives for visual information

## Provide Multiple Means of Action & Expression
*Strategic, goal-directed learners*

**Provide options for executive functions**
+ Guide appropriate goal-setting
+ Support planning and strategy development
+ Enhance capacity for monitoring progress

**Provide options for expression and communication**
+ Use multiple media for communication
+ Use multiple tools for construction and composition
+ Build fluencies with graduated levels of support for practice and performance

**Provide options for physical action**
+ Vary the methods for response and navigation
+ Optimize access to tools and assistive technologies

**FIGURE 7.6.** UDL Guidelines. © CAST, INC., 2014. USED WITH PERMISSION.

# Appendix

IN THE FOLLOWING PAGES, YOU'LL find templates and resources referenced throughout the book. We hope you'll find them helpful. They are, in order of reference:

Teachers: _____     School Year: _____

## Co-teaching Shared Vision Planning Page

Get your co-teaching year off to a strong start by sharing your views and then combining them into one shared vision for the year. Each co-teacher should write his or her response to each of the key questions. Once this page is complete, be sure to view this shared vision throughout the year so that you strengthen your co-actions and stay on track.

| | Co-teacher: | Co-teacher: |
|---|---|---|
| Name a few variables that support students' learning. | | |
| What is your view on the optimal classroom learning environment? | | |
| What talents do you bring as a teacher that you know can maximize the learning process for your students? | | |
| What is the best way to address students' learning differences? | | |

Combined Shared Vision:

© 2016 Elizabeth Stein

**FIGURE A.1.** Co-teaching Shared Vision Planning Page

Dear _____ :

   All co-teaching experiences range on a continuum between very awkward and unsuccessful to extremely cooperative, collaborative, and successful. All co-teaching experiences fall somewhere along this continuum of success. As you know, we are ready to do all we can to fall at the very successful end of the continuum. Yet we cannot do this alone. You can do a few things to support us as we strive to make this the most positive experience for our students and for ourselves.

## Creating a Building-Wide View of Variable Learners

Let's work together to redirect the thoughts that there are two teachers in the room because "some" students need extra help. Let's reframe these mind-sets and create a school culture where students, teachers, and parents accept that all learners are variable learners. Students with disabilities are part of this natural variability. Learner variability acknowledges that there is no such thing as the average learner—there is only variability. Let's support all students and not single any student out. This variability may be proactively planned for by designing instruction to meet the needs of each learner through using the UDL Guidelines as a framework for organizing our instruction so that each student may not only access the curriculum, but also meaningful connect, process, and apply their understandings.

## Creating a Culture of Collaboration

Let's make it a priority for us to have time to co-plan, to debrief, and to reflect. Each student in our room needs both of us to be on the same page. In addition, we need this co-planning time to work out any bumps in the road that will inevitably arise. In addition to our personal collaboration time, we need to connect with our colleagues. Let's find ways to naturally embed time for us to connect with other colleagues and support staff.

**FIGURE A.2.** Example Letter Showing Co-teachers' Communication with Principals

## Be a Part of our Team

We need you to be a part of our process. Please visit us in our classroom. Share your thoughts on what you notice in the classroom. What are we doing well? How can we improve? Your presence, support, and knowledge of our students and class routines will serve to empower us as we meet with any stumbling blocks along the way. Please use the Principal to Co-teachers Check-in to provide us with specific, objective feedback. We need this objective view!

Let's keep the communication open so that all of us remain focused and active along the path toward a successful co-teaching year! Thank you for all of your support.

Sincerely,

**FIGURE A.2 CONT.** Example Letter Showing Co-teachers' Communication with Principals

## Principal to Co-teachers Check-in

Co-teachers: _____ Principal: _____ Date: _____

This check-in is nonevaluative. The purpose is to guide both teachers toward strong parity and clearly defined roles in order to create a positive co-teaching environment. Each mark placed on the continuum for each question signifies what was noticed for this unannounced, quick check-in. The completed check-in should be used to guide the co-teachers in their professional growth, collaboration, and ultimately each student's personal achievements.

**1.** Both teachers were actively part of the learning process.

One teacher dominated while the other teacher quietly walked around the room.

Both teachers were active with clear, visible, role.

**2.** Students were engaged. This was evident because students were actively speaking, moving, and/or demonstrating their understanding.

Students were passively sitting at their seats for the most part.

Student voice and choice was evident.

© 2016 Elizabeth Stein

**FIGURE A.3.** Principal to Co-teachers Check-in

**3.** Instruction was clearly designed around the UDL principles with additional scaffolds to support students' IEP goals through specially designed instruction.

| | |
|---|---|
| Instruction was designed primarily around the curriculum. No evidence of UDL or co-teaching with SDI was seen during these moments. | Instruction was clearly designed to include the UDL principles. Additional supports were in place, so each learner had access and rigor. |

Thank you for welcoming me into your room. Please see the comments section for additional details and specific feedback.

Comments:

**FIGURE A.3 CONT.** Principal to Co-teachers Check-in

## Class Learning Profile

Teacher: _____  Class/Grade Level: _____  School Year: _____

| Network | Students' Strengths | Students' Needs | Students' Preferences/ Interests |
|---|---|---|---|
| Recognition (the "what" of learning) | | | |
| Strategic (the "how" of learning) | | | |
| Affect (the "why" of learning) | | | |

**FIGURE A.4.** Class Learning Profile Template

## Class Learning Profile

Teacher: __Ms. L._____ Class/Grade Level: __4th__ School Year: _____

| Network | Students' Strengths | Students' Needs | Students' Preferences/ Interests |
|---|---|---|---|
| Recognition (the "what" of learning) | *Anthony* Reads with expression<br>*Matthew* Enjoys opportunities to color or draw<br>*Rachel* Participates with support<br>*Teddy* Curious<br>*Michael* Organized<br>*Maria* Responds to commands when prompted or rewarded<br>*Marissa* Enjoys participating in class and especially enjoys having her voice heard | *Anthony* Needs to slow down<br>*Matthew* Comes to school tired; has low energy<br>*Rachel* Decoding, word recognition<br>*Teddy* Focuses on others, but needs to focus on himself<br>*Michael* Impulsive; needs self-control<br>*Maria* More independence, less prompting<br>*Marissa* Needs to remain focused on herself, not others<br>*Anthony* Cars | *Matthew* Drawing, dogs<br>*Rachel* Animals, the movie Frozen<br>*Teddy* Baseball, iPad<br>*Michael* Video games<br>*Maria* Predictable puzzles, snacks/foods<br>*Marissa* Dolls/stuffed animals |
| Strategic (the "how" of learning) | *Anthony* Enthusiastic about computer or iPad work<br>*Matthew* Enjoys illustrating<br>*Rachel* Works best in small groups or 1:1<br>*Teddy* Average in spelling skills<br>*Maria* Strengths in writing<br>*Marissa* Likes to feel like she's helping others | *Anthony* Poor handwriting<br>*Matthew* Rushes through work; wants others to believe he has finished first and/or convince others that he understands<br>*Rachel* Needs to apply reading strategies; does not participate in large-group discussions<br>*Teddy* Difficulty with written expression and multiple-step math problems<br>*Maria* Restless/fidgety; has difficulty paying attention<br>*Marissa* Speech impaired; fine motor delays; uses a pencil grip | |

**FIGURE A.5.** Class Learning Profile Sample

## Class Learning Profile

Teacher: __Ms. L._____ Class/Grade Level: __4th__ School Year: _____

| Network | Students' Strengths | Students' Needs | Students' Preferences/ Interests |
|---------|---------------------|-----------------|----------------------------------|
| Affect (the "why" of learning) | *Anthony* Willing to try new things; excited to begin new topics<br>*Matthew* Encourages others; has family support<br>*Rachel* Friendly, nurturing<br>*Teddy* Responds very well to classroom behavior plan<br>*Maria* High energy; tries hard to figure things out independently<br>*Marissa* Enjoys being called on by teacher | *Anthony* Needs to increase stamina<br>*Matthew* Easily confused by new concepts and directions; hard on himself, yet encourages others<br>*Rachel* Does not have support at home<br>*Teddy* Relies on others; does not complete work outside of school<br>*Maria* High energy; easily discouraged<br>*Marissa* Needs to accept constructive criticism; needs to be organized | |

**FIGURE A.5 CONT.** Class Learning Profile Sample

## Students—How to Annotate a Text:

1. Chunk the reading: read the text in manageable sections.

2. Ask yourself: Do I understand the reading so far? Write your questions in the margins.

3. Underline key words and phrases in each section.

4. Jot key words in margins.

5. Summarize your understanding through your choice: sketch, create a chart, write a short summary, or discuss the key ideas with peers.

**FIGURE A.6.** Student Application Cue Card

## How to Annotate a Text

1. Look closely at the text—notice its structure, style, context, imagery.

   - What does this section of reading make you think about?

   - What do you notice the author/poet does to help the readers understand what they are reading?

2. Notice what is said and how it is said. Underline, circle, and write in the margin. Make the text your own.

3. Jot down your thoughts in the margin by analyzing the text.

   - Write down what you notice.

   - Write down what you are thinking.

   - Paraphrase what you read in that section of the reading.


### Active Reading Actions:

Visualize
Connect
Infer
Predict
Question
Paraphrase
Evaluate

### Literary Devices to Notice:

Simile
Metaphor
Alliteration
Imagery
Personification
Tone (Author's Attitude)

**FIGURE A.7.** Teacher Modeling Cue Card

**Busting Co-teaching Barriers**
Creating a Clear Path to Learning for All Learners
Names of the co-teachers: _____

| Co-teaching Beliefs | Potential Barriers | Possible Solutions |
|---|---|---|
| What learning looks like in the co-taught classroom | | |
| Classroom management | | |
| Behavior management | | |
| Role of each teacher | | |

Adapted by E. Stein, April 2015
Original Source: Rose, D.H., & Meyer, A. (2002). Teaching every student in the digital age: Universal Design for Learning. Alexandria, VA: ASCD.

**FIGURE A.8.** Busting Co-teaching Barriers

Name:_____ Date: _____

## Strengths-Based Check-in Reflection

1. What is one personal strength that you feel proud of?

2. Describe one way you are effective in communicating with others—for example, speaking, listening, writing, telling stories, telling jokes, and so forth.

3. What are your social strengths? Examples include leadership abilities, helpful to others, socializing, and showing empathy for others.

4. What are your emotional strengths? Examples include positive attitude most of the time, able to push through struggles, accepts guidance from others, and cares for other people.

5. Name one intellectual strength that you have—for example, musical, artistic, creative, math, science, nature, reading, and writing.

6. Name one physical strength that you have—for example, exercise, bike riding, skateboarding, and sports.

7. Tell us more! What other strengths do you have? What hobbies do you have?

**FIGURE A.9.** Strengths-based Check-in Reflection

Dear Learners:

We are so excited to be your teachers this year! It is going to be an exciting year filled with curiosity and active learning. As a whole group, we create a community of learners where each voice matters! That means your voice is important as we create this comfortable learning environment.

So what do we mean by "your voice" anyway? Your voice is the thoughts you have quietly in your mind. It's the opinions, the connections, and the ideas that you think about as you observe your surroundings and participate in learning experiences. Your voice is unique to you—it is your ideas as you relate to the topics you will learn about this year.

Here are some ways you will strengthen your voice this year:

- You will begin to be more aware of what you think about the topics we discuss. That's right—your perspective is important!

- You will begin to be more comfortable sharing your thoughts with others. In addition to sharing your voice, you will listen to the voice of others. We will learn so much from one another.

- You may not always feel like sharing your thoughts out loud—and that's OK!

Here's what we, as your teachers will do to guide you to connect more closely with your voice—and with learning in general:

1. We will provide options for you to make decisions. For example, sometimes you will have a choice to work with a partner or work on your own. We will also teach you strategies that will help you to take charge of your own learning. We will always be here to help you, but you will learn ways to motivate and set yourself up to be motivated to learn.

2. We will provide a variety of ways to present material to you. For example, sometimes we will use videos, images, texts, audio, and class discussions.

**FIGURE A.10.** Letter to Learners

There will be times when you need to see what we're talking about. There will be other times when you need to listen, and yet other times when we will move around because that's the way you need to learn in those moments. So notice what works best for you—and tell us what you need!

3. We will provide many opportunities for you to collaborate with peers. You will learn strategies that work for you as you achieve your academic and personal goals. We will use a variety of tools, including technology, to communicate what we are learning. You will have a chance to speak, listen, write, sketch, and move about the room to express yourself!

We are looking forward to helping you to connect with who you are as a learner. This year will be an opportunity for you to not only value your voice, but also share it. We are looking forward to the process of you becoming your personal best this year!

Sincerely,

**FIGURE A.10 CONT.** Letter to Learners

Dear Parents/Caregivers:

As you know, we are part of a powerful co-teaching team that values the learning experiences of each learner in the room. In addition to optimizing learning by sharing our individual teaching expertise, we value the individual strengths, abilities, and thoughts that your child brings to our community of learners. Our classroom environment invites each student to take part in a meaningful learning process. Each learner has the opportunity to listen, speak, read, write, and express his or her thoughts in a variety of ways. Students are comfortable to value their own voice and share within a risk-free learning environment.

One main component that allows us to be flexible with our teaching and learning experiences is by applying Universal Design for Learning (UDL) within our daily routine.

UDL is a framework that taps into what brain research shows us to be true about how people learn. We know that as we focus on creating an accessible curriculum, each student in the classroom will connect personally with the content and the process of learning. This UDL mind-set empowers us to make the best instructional decisions possible for your children. Our UDL classroom naturally embeds the three principles that are essential for meaningful learning to take place.

1. **Multiple Means of Engagement:** Your child will experience learning as a purposeful, self-motivated learner. He or she will have opportunities to make choices, connect with peers through authentic collaborations and cooperative learning groups, and develop skills to strengthen his or her ability to self-regulate and motivate within a meaningful learning experience.

2. **Multiple Means of Representation:** Each week we will weave in a variety of ways to present information to our students. Your child will have the opportunity to perceive information in a variety of ways. For example, in addition to traditional text-based materials, we will be using digital tools to present

**FIGURE A.11.** Letter to Parents and Caregivers

information to provide alternatives to visual and auditory information. Your child will be guided to connect what he or she already knows to new concepts students will be learning. By the end of the school year, your child will become a more resourceful and knowledgeable learner.

3. Multiple Means of Action & Expression: We include options for communication throughout the year to maximize your child's ability to express his or her understanding. Through purposeful goal setting, your child will co-create and apply the action steps needed to become a strategic thinker who monitors his or her effort and progress throughout the learning process.

For more information about UDL, please visit the National Center on Universal Design for Learning at www.udlcenter.org/ and the Center for Applied Special Technology (CAST) at www.cast.org.

We are looking forward to a productive year of learning!

Sincerely,

**FIGURE A.11 CONT.** Letter to Parents and Caregivers

Name: _____  Date: _____

Text: _____  Pages: _____

Topic: _____

## Scan, Question, Read, Write

Scan:

- o  Read the title
- o  Introduction
- o  Headings
- o  Visuals
- o  Captions
- o  Bold print words

### Question Words:

Who    What    Where
When   Why     How

Question #1:

_____

_____

Write response #1:

_____

_____

Question #2:

_____

_____

Write response #2:

_____

_____

Question #3:

_____

_____

Write response #3:

_____

_____

**FIGURE A.12.** Scan–Question–Read–Write Template

Question #4:

_____

_____

Write response #4:

_____

_____

Question #5:

_____

_____

Write response #5:

_____

_____

**FIGURE A.12 CONT.** Scan–Question–Read–Write Template

# References

Armstrong, T. (2012). *Neurodiversity in the classroom: Strength-based strategies to help students with special needs succeed in school and life.* Alexandria, VA: Association for Supervision and Curriculum Development.

Blachowicz, C.L.Z. (1986). Making connections: Alternatives to the vocabulary notebook. *Journal of Reading 29,* 643–649.

Blackwell, L., Trzensniewski, K., & Dweck, C. (2007). Implicit theories of intelligence predict achievement across an adolescent transition: A longitudinal study and an intervention. *Child Development 78*(1), 246–263.

Carreker, S. (2004). *Developing metacognitive skills: Vocabulary and comprehension.* Bellaire, TX: Neuhaus Education Center.

CAST (2011). UDL Guidelines 2.0. Wakefield, MA: Author.

Collins, M., & Tamarkin, C. (1982). *Marva Collins' way.* Los Angeles, CA: J.P. Tarcher.

Dweck, C. (2006). *Mindset: The new psychology of success.* New York: Random House.

Ellis, E.S. (1999). *Using graphic organizers to make sense of the curriculum.* Tuscaloosa, AL: Masterminds.

Friend, M. (2014). *Co-teach! Creating and sustaining effective classroom partnerships in inclusive schools* (2nd ed.). Greensboro, NC: Marilyn Friend, Inc.

Friend, M. & Cook, L. (2007). *Interactions: Collaboration skills for school professionals* (5th ed.). Boston, MA: Pearson/Allyn & Bacon.

Gargiulo, R.M., & Metcalf, D.J. (2013). *Teaching in today's inclusive classrooms: A universal design for learning approach* (2nd ed.). Belmont, CA: Wadsworth Cengage Learning.

Harvey, S., & Goudvis, A. (2000). *Strategies that work: Teaching comprehension to enhance understanding.* Portland, ME: Stenhouse.

Kalam, A., & Tiwari, A. (1999). *Wings of fire: An autobiography.* Hyderabad, A.P., India: Universities Press.

Klingner, J.K. & Vaughn, S. (1999). Promoting reading comprehension, content learning, and English acquisition through Collaborative Strategic Reading (CSR). *The Reading Teacher 52*(7), 738–747.

Lansdown, S. (1991). Increasing vocabulary knowledge using direct instruction, cooperative grouping, and reading in junior high school. *Illinois Reading Council Journal 19*, 15–21.

Strichart, S., & Mangrum, C. (2002). *Teaching learning strategies and skills to students with learning disabilities, attention deficit disorders, or special needs.* Boston: Allyn & Bacon.

Meyer, A., Rose, D.H., & Gordon, D. (2014). *Universal design for learning: Theory and practice.* Wakefield, MA: CAST Professional Publishing.

Palincsar, A.M., & Brown, A.L. (1984). Reciprocal teaching of comprehension-fostering and comprehension-monitoring activities. *Cognition and Instruction 1*(2), 117–175.

Pintrich, P.R., & Zusho, A. (2002). The development of academic self-regulation: The role of cognitive and motivational factors. In A. Wigfield, & J.S. Eccles (Eds.), *Development of achievement motivation* (pp. 249–284). San Diego, CA: Academic Press.

Reynolds, P.H. (2004). *Ish.* Somerville, MA: Candlewick.

Reynolds, P.H. (2009). *The North Star.* Somerville, MA: Candlewick.

Robinson, K. (2014). The art of teaching (video). Learning (Re)imagined (website). Retrieved from http://learning-reimagined.com/sir-ken-robinson-art-of-teaching/ (accessed June 13, 2016).

Rose, D.H., & Meyer, A. (2002). *Teaching every student in the digital age: Universal Design for Learning.* Alexandria, VA: Association for Supervision and Curriculum Development.

Rose, T. (2011). Learner variability and UDL (Universal Design for Learning Series). Wakefield, MA: National Center on Universal Design for Learning.

Sabia, R. (2008). Universal Design for Learning and meaningful access to the curriculum. *TASH Connections,* May/June, 14–21.

Tomlinson, C. (1999). Mapping a route toward differentiated instruction. *Educational Leadership 57*(1), 12–16.

Vacca, R.T., & Vacca, J.L. (1986). *Content area reading.* New York: Little, Brown.

Vygotsky, L.S. (1978). *Mind in society: The development of higher psychological processes.* Cambridge, MA: Harvard University Press.

Willingham, Daniel T. (2009). *Why don't students like school?* San Francisco, CA: Jossey-Bass.

# Index

co-teaching tips
    and accountable talk, 142
    brainstorming breaks, 127
    card pyramid, 138
    choice boards, 125
    choice of assessment, 126
    concept circles, 140
    connect, collect, correct, 137
    CSR (collaborative strategic
        reading), 133
    exclusion brainstorming, 141
    flex-time, 130
    FQR (Fact, Question,
        Response), 136
    and gallery walk, 150
    and get up and go, 146
    hint cards, 129
    interactive notebooks, 134
    Lansdown word cards, 143
    and learning links, 151
    and line-ups, 152
    and paraphrasing ticket, 149
    and peer-to-peer think-aloud, 148
    and points to ponder, 147
    QAD (Question-Answer-Detail), 136
    seat selection, 124–125
    student inquiry teams, 128
    and text on text, 145
CSR (collaborative strategic reading),
    133. See also reading
cue cards for annotating text, 164–165
curriculum
    components of, 68
    planning, 38
    UDL versus traditional approach,
        69–73

## D

deficit-model barrier, breaking through,
    46–47

depth of coverage, increasing,
    58–59, 117
DI (differentiated instruction), 51–53
diverse learners. See learner variability
Dweck, Carol, 28

## E

education, general versus special, 9
effort and persistence, sustaining,
    78, 154
Ellis, Edwin, 58, 116
emotions, role in learning, 21
engagement, 34
    and accountable talk, 142
    and brain networks, 41
    and brainstorming breaks, 127
    card pyramid, 138
    and choice boards, 125
    and choice of assessment, 126
    concept circles, 139
    connect, collect, correct, 137
    and co-teaching effectiveness,
        92–93
    and CSR (collaborative strategic
        reading), 133
    evidence in co-taught classrooms,
        102–103
    exclusion brainstorming, 140
    and expert learners, 27
    and flex-time, 130
    and FQR (Fact, Question,
        Response), 136
    and gallery walk, 149
    and get up and go, 146
    and hint cards, 129
    and interactive notebooks, 134
    Lansdown word cards, 143
    and learner variability, 23–24
    and learning links, 150
    and line-ups, 151

and SDI (specially designed instruction), 49–50

UDL Guidelines, 51–56

instructional improvement, phases of, 82

instructional materials, 68, 70–71

instructional process, 82

interactive notebooks, 134

interest. *See* recruiting interest

*Ish*, 109

## K

Kalam, Abdul, 108

Klingner & Vaughn, 133

knowledge
    connections, 59, 117
    constructing, 58, 116

knowledgeable learners, 34, 154

## L

language, providing options for, 35, 154

Lansdown word cards, 143

learner variability. *See also* expert learners; variable learners
    and neuroscience, 24
    overview, 19–22
    and UDL, 22–25
    and UDL (Universal Design for Learning), 22–25

learners. *See also* students
    building self-awareness in, 36
    including in co-teaching team, 114–116
    keeping expectations high for, 58–61
    types of, 34, 154

learners' independence, scaffolding, 115

learning. *See also* Class Learning Profile
    context of, 31
    toward independence, 57

learning goals, clarity of, 67

learning links, 150–151

learning networks, 38

learning process, phases of, 111

learning profile, 161–163

learning strategies, developing habits of, 61, 119

learning styles, avoiding talking about, 30–31

Letter to Learners, 168–169

Letter to Parents and Caregivers, 170–171

line-ups, 151–152

listening and speaking. *See* peer collaboration

literacy devices, noting, 165

London, Jack, 75

## M

*Martin Eden*, 75

materials in curriculum, 68, 70–71

mathematical expressions, providing options for, 35, 154

methods in curriculum, 68

Meyer, Rose, and Gordon, 21

Michael's examples, 90–91, 95

mind, developing habits of, 61, 119

mind-sets, defined, 28. *See also* UDL mind-set

motivated learners, 34, 154

motivation to learn, increasing, 57–58

Ms. A. and Ms. C. scenario, 29–30

Ms. Fields scenario, 88

Ms. M. scenario, 14

## N

neuroscience and learner variability, 24

notebooks. *See* interactive notebooks

note-taking organizer, 88, 136–137

Westward Expansion concept
   circle, 139
"what" of learning, 38
"why" of learning, 38
Willingham, Daniel, 30
words. *See* vocabulary words
workshop structure, applying, 114–116

## Y

"You Do!" in workshop structure, 115–116

## Z

ZAD (zone of actual development), 114–115
ZPD (zone of proximal development),
   56, 115

# Acknowledgements

ALL ORIGINAL AND CREATIVE WORK IS THE RESULT OF THE EVOLVING IDEAS SHARED BETWEEN INNOVATIVE THINKERS OVER TIME—AND THIS BOOK IS NO EXCEPTION. This book has a solid foundation in the works of great theorists and researchers, past and present.

The works of Lev Vygotsky, Jerome Bruner, Benjamin Bloom, and John Dewey have a clear voice throughout these pages.

Present educational thinkers and doers such as Carol Dweck, Marilyn Friend, Daniel Willingham, Thomas Armstrong, and Howard Gardner weave a strong influence throughout my daily instructional decisions—as well as within the composition of this book.

The strongest influence on my daily instructional decisions and my thinking while writing this book has come from the work of David Rose, Todd Rose, Grace Meo, and everyone involved with CAST. These innovative minds share what has been so common sense to me since I began teaching 25 years ago. Their hard work, dedication, and research have been the mainstay that supported my focus and mission over the decades.

A heartfelt thank you finds its way to David Gordon at CAST Professional Publishing for our engaging conversations and his insightful writing and editing guidance. With the wise and objective vision of editor Billie Fitzpatrick, I found another way to organize the book's structure and voice—thank you for your editing magic. Thanks, too, to the team at Happenstance Type-O-Rama for their beautiful design and expert production.

The collaborations and voices of so many colleagues over the years have given me the opportunities to strengthen my UDL voice and to exercise the patience, perseverance, compassion, and tenacity needed to keep students at the center of the learning process in all situations.

Additional appreciation goes out to all administrators I have had the pleasure of learning from and with through the years—with a shared vision and mission, we raised and maintained high expectations for all learners.

My gratitude reaches new levels as I thank Jennifer Bradshaw, assistant superintendent for instruction, and Paul Strader, executive director of curriculum at the Smithtown Central School District, who not only provide the space and time for me to live out my UDL dream as our district's special education/UDL instructional coach, but who also trust and support me as I do my share to sprinkle the UDL magic throughout our school district.

To all of my past, present, and future students: It is from you that I truly learn how powerful UDL can be. You show us all how to implement UDL in the most meaningful ways possible.

To my family—you are my true anchor, my equanimous breath, the center of my universe.

# About the Author

ELIZABETH STEIN'S career includes experiences spanning early intervention, grades K-12, and under-graduate and graduate level education courses. She is a special education teacher and UDL coach in Long Island's Smithtown Central School District.

She is a contributing writer to *Education Week* and the author of a popular blog, Two Teachers in the Room, at MiddleWeb. Her first book, *Comprehension Lessons for RTI: Grades 3-5: Assessments, Intervention Lessons, and Management Tips to Help You Reach and Teach Tier 2* was published by Scholastic in 2013.

Elizabeth earned her National Board Certification in Literacy and is a doctoral student at Molloy College's Educational Leadership for Diverse Learning Communities program.

Follow her on Twitter *@ElizabethLStein*.